CSS3 AND SVG
WITH GEMINI

CSS3 AND SVG
WITH GEMINI

OSWALD CAMPESATO

MERCURY LEARNING AND INFORMATION
Boston, Massachusetts

Publisher: David Pallai
MERCURY LEARNING AND INFORMATION
121 High Street, 3rd Floor
Boston, MA 02110
info@merclearning.com
www.merclearning.com
800-232-0223

O. Campesato. *CSS3 and SVG Using Gemini.*
ISBN: 978-1-50152-293-2

The publisher recognizes and respects all marks used by companies, manufacturers, and developers as a means to distinguish their products. All brand names and product names mentioned in this book are trademarks or service marks of their respective companies. Any omission or misuse (of any kind) of service marks or trademarks, etc. is not an attempt to infringe on the property of others.

Library of Congress Control Number: 2024935760

242526321   This book is printed on acid-free paper in the United States of America.

Our titles are available for adoption, license, or bulk purchase by institutions, corporations, etc. For additional information, please contact the Customer Service Dept. at 800-232-0223(toll free).

I'd like to dedicate this book to my parents
– may this bring joy and happiness into their lives.

CONTENTS

**CHAPTER 7: SCALABLE VECTOR GRAPHICS (SVG)
AND GEMINI**   **163**

PREFACE

Preface

This book provides code samples involving graphics-based Web development and artificial intelligence (AI). We focus on various aspects of modern web development and AI technologies, with a particular emphasis on Generative AI, Google Gemini, CSS3, and SVG, which includes features such as 3D animations and gradient effects. By exploring these topics, readers will gain a deeper understanding of how AI can enhance web development processes and how to leverage AI models like Gemini to streamline development workflows.

Intended Audience

Whether you are a seasoned web developer looking to stay ahead in the AI-focused world or a beginner eager to explore the possibilities of AI-driven web development, this book is for you. Web developers, UI/UX designers, and software engineers seeking to blend traditional web development skills with the latest AI technologies will find this book to be a valuable resource.

Chapter Summaries

Chapter 1: Generative AI and Gemini: We introduce Generative AI, exploring its key features, applications, and prominent players like DeepMind and OpenAI. Additionally, we introduce Gemini, Google's innovative model, discussing its strengths, weaknesses, and its various versions.

Chapter 2: Prompt Engineering: Discussing the intricacies of prompt engineering, this chapter provides an in-depth overview of different prompt types, their importance, and guidelines for effective prompt design, essential for optimal interaction with AI models like Gemini.

Chapter 3: Introduction to CSS3: Here, we lay the foundation of CSS3, covering its features, browser support, and essential concepts like shadow effects, gradients, and 2D transforms. We also address security and accessibility concerns, ensuring a holistic understanding of CSS3 principles.

Chapter 4: CSS3 3D Animation: Building upon CSS3 fundamentals, this chapter explores advanced topics such as 3D animation effects, transitions, and media queries. Through practical examples, readers learn to create animations using CSS3 techniques.

Chapter 5: CSS3 and Gemini: Focusing on the integration of CSS3 with Gemini, this chapter demonstrates how Gemini-generated code can enhance web design. Readers explore various CSS3 use cases, security considerations, and sample code generated by Gemini.

Chapter 6: Introduction to Scalable Vector Graphics(SVG): Introducing Scalable Vector Graphics (SVG), this chapter covers basic shapes, gradients, transformations, and animation techniques. Readers gain insights into leveraging SVG for creating dynamic and responsive visuals.

Chapter 7: Scalable Vector Graphics (SVG) and Gemini: Finally, we look at the synergy between SVG and Gemini, highlighting their combined potential for web development. From linear gradients to complex animations, readers learn to harness the power of SVG alongside Gemini-generated content.

Key Features of the Book

- *Comprehensive Coverage:* From AI fundamentals to advanced CSS3 and SVG techniques, this book offers a comprehensive exploration of modern web development technologies.

- *Practical Insights:* With a balance of theoretical knowledge and practical examples, readers gain hands-on experience in implementing AI-driven design solutions using Gemini-generated code.

- *Companion files:* Files with source code, datasets, and images from the book are available from the publisher for downloading (with proof of purchase).

What Do I Need to Know?

The most useful prerequisite is some familiarity with another scripting language, such as JavaScript, Perl, or PHP. The less technical knowledge that you have, the more diligence will be required in order to understand the various topics that are covered. If you want to be sure that you can grasp the material in this book, glance through some of the code samples to get an idea of what is familiar to you and what is new for you.

About the Cover

The cover image was generated using DALL-E with the following:

Prompt: "Please render buildings that have structures that are similar to cubic Bezier curves."

Response (with image):

"Here is the image of a futuristic building inspired by cubic Bezier curves, with smooth, flowing, and curvilinear designs, set in a modern cityscape."

As you explore the subjects of web development and AI, I encourage you to engage actively with the content, experiment with code samples, and embrace the opportunities that AI-driven web development presents. This book will guide you every step of the way.

O. Campesato
May 2024

CHAPTER

1

GENERATIVE AI AND GEMINI

This chapter provides an overview of GenAI and Google Gemini, along with the main features of Gemini Ultra and Gemini Pro.

The first section of this chapter starts with information about key features of GenAI, as well as a comparison of generative AI and conversational AI.

The second section of this chapter discusses some of the main companies that are involved in GenAI, such as DeepMind, OpenAI, Cohere, and Hugging Face.

The third section discusses prompt engineering, which includes a description of various techniques that you can use in prompt engineering. Moreover, you will see examples of prompts to avoid when you are working with LLMs (large language models).

The fourth section of this chapter provides an overview of Gemini, which includes a description of the three models Ultra, Pro, and Nano.

With the preceding details in mind, let's proceed to a description of Generative AI, which is the topic of the next section.

WHAT IS GENERATIVE AI?

Generative AI refers to a subset of artificial intelligence models and techniques that are designed to generate new data samples that are similar in nature to a given set of input data. The goal is to produce content or data that wasn't part of the original training set but is coherent, contextually relevant, and in the same style or structure.

Generative AI stands apart in its ability to create and innovate, as opposed to merely analyzing or classifying. The advancements in this field have led to breakthroughs in creative domains and practical applications, making it a cutting-edge area of AI research and development.

Key Features of Generative AI

The following bullet list contains key features of generative AI, followed by a brief description for each bullet item:

- data generation
- synthesis
- learning distributions
- learning distributions

Data generation refers to the ability to create new data points that are not part of the training data but resemble it. This can include text, images, music, videos, or any other form of data.

Synthesis indicates generative models can blend various inputs to generate outputs that incorporate features from each input, for example, merging the styles of two images.

Learning distributions means that generative AI models aim to learn the probability distribution of the training data so they can produce new samples from that distribution.

Popular Techniques in Generative AI

Generative adversarial networks (GANs): GANs consist of two networks, a generator and a discriminator, that are trained simultaneously. The generator tries to produce fake data, while the discriminator tries to distinguish between real data and fake data. Over time, the generator gets better at producing realistic data.

Variational autoencoders (VAEs): VAEs are probabilistic models that learn to encode and decode data in a manner in which the encoded representations can be used to generate new data samples.

Recurrent neural networks (RNNs): Used primarily for sequence generation, such as text or music.

What Makes Generative AI Different

Creation versus Classification: While most traditional AI models aim to classify input data into predefined categories, generative models aim to create new data.

Unsupervised learning: Many generative models, especially GANs and VAEs, operate in an unsupervised manner, meaning they don't require labeled data for training.

Diverse outputs: Generative models can produce a wide variety of outputs based on learned distributions, making them ideal for tasks like art generation, style transfer, and more.

Challenges: Generative AI poses unique challenges, such as mode collapse in GANs or ensuring the coherence of generated content.

Furthermore, there are numerous areas that involve generative AI applications, some of which are listed in the following bullet list:

- art and music creation
- data augmentation
- style transfer
- text generation
- image synthesis

Art and music creation includes generating paintings, music, or other forms of art.

Data augmentation involves creating additional data for training models, especially when the original dataset is limited.

Style transfer refers to applying the style of one image to the content of another.

Text generation is a very popular application of generative AI, which involves creating coherent and contextually relevant text.

Image synthesis is another popular area of generative AI, which involves generating realistic images, faces, or even creating scenes for video games.

Drug discovery is a very important facet of generative AI that pertains to generating molecular structures for new potential drugs.

CONVERSATIONAL AI VERSUS GENERATIVE AI

Both conversational AI and generative AI are prominent subfields within the broader domain of artificial intelligence. However, these subfields have a different focus regarding their primary objective as well as the technologies that they use.

Information about those differences can be found here: *https://medium. com/@social_65128/differences-between-conversational-ai-and-generative-ai-e3adca2a8e9a*

The primary differences between the two subfields are in the following sequence of bullet points:

- primary objective
- applications
- technologies used
- training and interaction
- evaluation
- data requirements

Primary Objective

The main goal of conversational AI is to facilitate human-like interactions between machines and humans. This includes chatbots, virtual assistants, and other systems that engage in dialogue with users.

The primary objective of generative AI is to create new content or data that wasn't in the training set but is similar in structure and style. This can range from generating images, music, and text to more complex tasks like video synthesis.

Applications

Common applications for conversational AI include customer support chatbots, voice-operated virtual assistants (like Siri or Alexa), and interactive voice response (IVR) systems.

Common applications for generative AI include a broad spectrum of applications such as creating art or music, generating realistic video game environments, synthesizing voices, and producing realistic images or even deep fakes.

Technologies Used

Conversational AI often relies on natural language processing (NLP) techniques to understand and generate human language. This includes intent recognition, entity extraction, and dialogue management.

Generative AI commonly utilizes GANs, VAEs, and other generative models to produce new content.

Training and Interaction

While training can be supervised, semi-supervised, or unsupervised, the primary interaction mode for conversational AI is through back-and-forth dialogue or conversation.

The training process for generative AI, especially with models like GANs, involves iterative processes where the model learns to generate data by trying to fool a discriminator into believing the generated data is real.

Evaluation

Conversational AI evaluation metrics often revolve around understanding and response accuracy, user satisfaction, and the fluency of generated responses.

Generative AI evaluation metrics for models like GANs can be challenging and might involve using a combination of quantitative metrics and human judgment to assess the quality of generated content.

Data Requirements

Data requirements for conversational AI typically involves dialogue data, with conversations between humans or between humans and bots.

Data requirements for generative AI involve large datasets of the kind of content it is supposed to generate, be it images, text, music, and so on.

Although both conversational AI and generative AI deal with generating outputs, their primary objectives, applications, and methodologies can differ significantly. Conversational AI is geared toward interactive communication with users, while generative AI focuses on producing new, original content.

IS GEMINI PART OF GENERATIVE AI?

Gemini is an LLM that is considered part of generative AI. Gemini belongs to a class of models called "transformers" that are particularly adept at handling sequences of data, such as text-related tasks.

The following bullet list provides various reasons why Gemini is considered generative, followed by a brief description of each bullet item:

- text generation
- learning distributions
- broad applications
- unsupervised learning

Text generation: These models can produce coherent, contextually relevant, and often highly sophisticated sequences of text based on given prompts. They generate responses that weren't explicitly present in their training data but are constructed based on the patterns and structures they learned during training.

Learning distributions: Gemini (as well as GPT-3, GPT-4, and similar models) learn the probability distribution of their training data. When generating text, they're essentially sampling from this learned distribution to produce sequences that are likely based on their training.

Broad applications: Beyond just text-based chat or conversation, these models can be used for a variety of generative tasks like story writing, code generation, poetry, and even creating content in specific styles or mimicking certain authors, showcasing their generative capabilities.

Unsupervised learning: While they can be fine-tuned with specific datasets, models like GPT-3 are primarily trained in an unsupervised manner on vast amounts of text, learning to generate content without requiring explicit labeled data for every possible response.

In essence, Google Gemini is a quintessential example of generative AI in the realm of natural language processing and generation.

The next several sections briefly introduce some of the companies that have a strong presence in the AI world.

DEEPMIND

DeepMind (*https://deepmind.com/*) has made significant contributions to artificial intelligence, which includes the creation of various AI systems. DeepMind was established in 2010 and became a subsidiary of Google in 2014. DeepMind created the 280GB language model `Gopher` that significantly outperforms its competitors, including GPT-3, `J1-Jumbo`, and `MT-NLG`. DeepMind also developed `AlphaFold` that solved a protein folding task in literally 30 minutes that had eluded researchers for ten years. Moreover, DeepMind made `AlphaFold` available for free for everyone in July 2021. DeepMind has made significant contributions in the development of world caliber AI game systems, some of which are discussed in the next section.

DeepMind and Games

DeepMind is the force behind the `AI` systems `StarCraft` and `AlphaGo` that defeated the best human players in `Go` (which is considerably more difficult than chess). These games provide "perfect information," whereas games with "imperfect information" (such as Poker) have posed a challenge for ML models.

`AlphaGo Zero` (the successor of `AlphaGo`) mastered the game through self-play in less time and with less computing power. `AlphaGo Zero` exhibited extraordinary performance by defeating `AlphaGo` 100–0. Another powerful system is `AlphaZero` that also used a self-play technique learned to play Go, chess, and shogi, and also achieved SoTA (State of the Art) performance results.

By way of comparison, ML models that use tree search are well-suited for games with perfect information. By contrast, games with imperfect information (such as Poker) involve hidden information that can be leveraged to devise counter strategies to counteract the strategies of opponents. In particular, `AlphaStar` is capable of playing against the best players of `StarCraft II`, and also became the first AI to achieve SoTA results in a game that requires "strategic capability in an imperfect information world."

Player of Games (PoG)

The DeepMind team at Google devised the general-purpose PoG (player of games) algorithm that is based on the following techniques:

- CFR (counterfactual regret minimization)
- CVPN (counterfactual value-and-policy network)
- GT-CFT (growing tree CFR)
- CVPN

The counterfactual value-and-policy network (CVPN) is a neural network that calculates the counterfactuals for each state belief in the game. This is key to evaluating the different variants of the game at any given time.

Growing tree CFR (GT-CFR) is a variation of CFR that is optimized for game-trees trees that grow over time. GT-CFR is based on two fundamental phases, which is discussed in more detail here:

https://medium.com/syncedreview/deepminds-pog-excels-in-perfect-and-imperfect-information-games-advancing-research-on-general-9dbad5c04221

OPENAI

OpenAI (*https://openai.com/api/*) is an AI research company that has made significant contributions to AI, including DALL-E and GPT-4.

OpenAI was founded in San Francisco by Elon Musk and Sam Altman (and others), and one of its stated goals is to develop AI that benefits humanity. Given Microsoft's massive investments in and deep alliance with the organization, OpenAI might be viewed as an arm of Microsoft. OpenAI is the creator of the GPT-x series of LLMs (large language models) as well as ChatGPT that was made available on November 30, 2022.

In addition, OpenAI developed DALL-E that generates images from text. OpenAI initially did not permit users to upload images that contained realistic faces. Later (Q4/2022) OpenAI changed its policy to allow users to upload faces into its online system. Check the OpenAI Web page for more details.

OpenAI has also released a public beta of `Embeddings`, which is a data format that is suitable for various types of tasks with machine learning, as described here: *https://beta.openai.com/docs/guides/embeddings*

OpenAI is the creator of Codex that provides a set of models that were trained on NLP. The initial release of Codex was in private beta, and more information is accessible here: *https://beta.openai.com/docs/engines/instruct-series-beta*

OpenAI provides four models that are collectively called their Instruct models, which support the ability of GPT-3 to generate natural language. These models were deprecated in early January 2024 and replaced with an updated versions of GPT-3, ChatGPT, and GPT-4.

If you want to learn more about the features and services that OpenAI offers, navigate to the following link: *https://platform.openai.com/overview*

COHERE

Cohere (*https://cohere.ai/*) is a start-up and a competitor of Gemini as well as GPT-4.

Cohere develops cutting-edge NLP technology that is commercially available for multiple industries. Cohere is focused on models that perform textual analysis instead of models for text generation (such as GPT-based models). The founding team of Cohere is impressive: CEO Aidan Gomez is one of the co-inventors of the transformer architecture, and CTO Nick Frost is a protégé of Geoff Hinton.

HUGGING FACE

Hugging Face (*https://github.com/huggingface*) is a popular community-based repository for open-source NLP technology. Unlike OpenAI or Cohere, Hugging Face does not build its own NLP models. Instead, Hugging Face is a platform that manages a plethora of open-source NLP models that customers can fine-tune and then deploy those fine-tuned models. Indeed, Hugging Face has become the eminent location for people to collaborate on NLP models, and sometimes described as "GitHub for machine learning and NLP."

Hugging Face Libraries

Hugging Face provides three important libraries: datasets, tokenizers for LLMs, and transformers (discussed in Chapter 3). The Accelerate library supports `PyTorch` models. The datasets library provides an assortment of libraries for NLP. The tokenizers library enables you to convert text data to numeric values.

Perhaps the most impressive library is the transformers library that provides an enormous set of pretrained `BERT`-based models (discussed in Chapter 5) in order to perform a wide variety of NLP tasks. The Github repository is here: *https://github.com/huggingface/transformers*

Hugging Face Model Hub

Hugging Face provides a model hub that provides a plethora of models that are accessible online. Moreover, the Web site supports online testing of its models, which includes the following tasks:

- masked word completion with BERT
- name entity recognition with Electra
- natural language inference with RoBERTa
- question answering with DistilBERT
- summarization with BART
- text generation with GPT-2
- translation with T5

Navigate to the following link to see the text generation capabilities of "write with transformer:" *https://transformer.huggingface.co*

In a subsequent chapter you will see Python code samples that show how to list all the available Hugging Face datasets and also how to load a specific dataset.

AI21

AI21 is a company that provides proprietary LLMs via API to support the applications of its customers. The current SoTA model of AI21 is called `Jurassic-1` (roughly the same size as GPT-3), and AI21 also creates its own applications on top of `Jurassic-1` and other models. The current application suite of AI21 involves tools that can augment reading and writing.

`Primer` is an older competitor in this space, founded two years before the invention of the transformer. The company primarily serves clients in government and defense.

ANTHROPIC

Anthropic (*https://www.anthropic.com/*) was created in 2021 by former employees of OpenAI.

Anthropic has significant financial support from an assortment of companies, including Google and Salesforce. Anthropic released Claude 2 as a competitor to ChatGPT.

Claude 2 has the ability to summarize as much as 75,000 words of text-based content. Moreover, Claude 2 achieved a score of 76.5% on portions of the bar exam and 71% in a Python coding test. Claude 2 also has a higher rate than Gemini in terms of providing "clean" responses to queries from users.

This concludes the portion of the chapter regarding the AI companies that are making important contributions in AI. The next section provides a high-level introduction to LLMs.

WHAT IS GOOGLE GEMINI?

Gemini is the most advanced LLM from Google. In addition, Gemini is available in three sizes: Ultra (released on February 8, 2024) is the most advanced, Pro (replacement for Bard), and Nano for mobile devices (such as Pixel 8).

Gemini is a multimodal LLM that can process various types of input, including text, code, audio, images and videos. Specifically, Gemini generated some of the Python code samples in Chapters 3 and 4, as well as all the Python code samples in Chapter 6. However, some of the multimodal features of Gemini will become available at a later point in time. Gemini also sometimes suffers from so-called "hallucinations," which is common for LLMs.

Gemini Ultra Versus GPT-4

Google performed a comparison of Gemini Ultra and GPT-4 from OpenAI, and Ultra outperformed GPT-4 on seven of eight text-based tests. Moreover, Ultra outperformed GPT-4 on ten out of ten multimodal tests.

In many cases, Ultra outperformed GPT-4 by a fairly small margin, which means that both LLMs are competitive in terms of functionality. Note that thus far Google has not provided a comparison of Gemini Pro or Gemini Nano with GPT-4.

Gemini's Strengths

Accuracy and factuality: Gemini is trained on a massive dataset of text and code, including factual information from Google Search. This allows it to provide accurate and reliable answers to factual questions.

Comprehensiveness: Gemini provides more comprehensive and detailed answers compared to other LLMss. It retrieves relevant information from its database and presents it in a clear and concise manner.

User-friendly interface: Gemini has a user-friendly interface that is easy to navigate and use. It allows users to edit their questions, upvote and downvote responses, and search for information on the Web.

Multiple response formats: Gemini can generate text in various formats, including poems, code, scripts, musical pieces, emails, letters, and more. This makes it versatile and adaptable to different tasks.

Free to use: Gemini is currently free to use, which makes it accessible to a wider audience.

Gemini's Weaknesses

The following paragraphs contain a description of some of the perceived weaknesses of Gemini, half of which are somewhat subjective in nature.

Lack of creativity: While Gemini can generate creative text formats, it sometimes lacks originality and can be repetitive. It struggles with tasks that require a high level of imagination and out-of-the-box thinking.

Poor conversational flow: Gemini can sometimes be clunky and unnatural in conversation. Its responses may not always flow smoothly or follow the context of the conversation.

Deficient technical knowledge: Although trained on a massive dataset, Gemini can struggle with technical questions or tasks that require specialized knowledge in specific domains.

Limited integrations: Compared to ChatGPT, Gemini has fewer integrations with other apps and services. This limits its functionality and flexibility.

Limited customizability: Users currently have limited options to customize Gemini's behavior or preferences.

Gemini Nano on Mobile Devices

Gemini Nano provides features such as grammar correction, proofreading, and text summarization. Moreover, a software update for Pixel 8 Pro is available in order to provide access to Gemini Nano on this mobile device. Other features will be supported on mobile devices in the coming months.

Google has also created Android AICore, which is a system service that provides access to Nano on Android devices. This service supports improved safety and model management in a manner that makes it easier for you to incorporate AI into Android devices.

GEMINI 1.5 AND GEMINI 1.0

Google Gemini 1.0 was released on February 8, 2024, followed by Google Gemini 1.5 on February 15, 2024. Version 1.5 is recommended because it's touted as substantively better than version 1.0.

We will look at the list of features of version 1.5 and then delve into more detail for version 1.0, right after we discuss the three models that are available in both versions of Google Gemini in the next section.

The Three Models of Google Gemini

Google Gemini consists of three models: Gemini Ultra (the most advanced), Gemini Pro (available in Bard), and Gemini Nano (for mobile devices).

Ultra was available for free for two months following its initial launch date. It is currently available by subscription at the cost of $19.99 per month. Google Pro is currently available as a free option, or by subscription at the cost of $19.19 per month.

Features of Google Gemini 1.5

Although Google Gemini 1.5 is currently in a private beta mode, it's possible to obtain information about its features by supplying the following prompt to Gemini Ultra:

```
Prompt: Please provide a list of features of Gemini Ultra.

Ultra: Absolutely! Here's a breakdown of Gemini Ultra's key
features:
```

1. **Advanced Reasoning and Problem Solving**
   - **Complex Analysis:** Gemini Ultra excels in understanding and breaking down intricate concepts, drawing inferences, and finding insightful connections across vast domains of information.
   - **Multimodal Understanding:** It can process and reason across images, text, and code simultaneously, making its responses more comprehensive and helpful. For example, it could analyze a photo, provide a descriptive summary, and generate code to recreate the image.

2. **Enhanced Creativity**

  · **Content Creation:** Not just text-based responses, Gemini Ultra helps brainstorm ideas, drafts different creative text formats (emails, poems, scripts, musical pieces, etc.), and translates between languages.

  · **Code Generation:** It can write and debug different code formats, potentially offering helpful solutions for developers.

3. **Up-to-Date and Informative**

  · **Real-World Knowledge:** Gemini Ultra stays current by accessing and processing real-world information. This means more relevant and factual responses.

  · **Summarization:** It can efficiently summarize long documents, articles, or conversations, extracting the most important points.

4. **Tailored to Your Needs**

  · **Adaptability:** Gemini Ultra learns and adapts to your style and preferences over time, making future interactions even more seamless and personalized.

  · **Systematic Learning:** It can break down tasks, provide step-by-step instructions, and offer guidance to help you master new skills or concepts more effectively.

5. **Important Notes:**

  · Gemini Ultra is constantly evolving, so even more capabilities are likely to be added.

  · Google aims to make Gemini Ultra widely accessible, including integration into Google products like Search, Google Workspace, and more.

Let me know if you'd like more details on any specific feature!

Now let's turn our attention to Google Gemini 1.0, which is the topic of the next section.

Features of Google Gemini 1.0

The following prompt was supplied to Gemini Ultra to describe Gemini, along with the functionality that is available in Gemini.

```
Please provide a detailed description of the features of
Gemini, along with its functionality.
```

Here's a detailed look at Gemini's features and capabilities:

Core Abilities

  · **Multimodality:** One of Gemini's hallmarks is its ability to understand and reason across different modalities like text, images, videos, code, and audio. This means it can analyze a picture and generate a caption, understand a code snippet, or follow instructions that combine textual and visual elements.

- **Reasoning and Problem-Solving:** Gemini goes beyond information retrieval. It can synthesize information, make inferences, and provide step-by-step explanations for its reasoning. This makes it well-suited for tasks that require logic or sequential thinking.
- **Advanced Information Retrieval:** Gemini draws on a vast knowledge base to answer complex factual questions, provide summaries on nuanced topics, and conduct deep research dives with more accuracy than previous models.
- **Creative Capabilities:** Gemini can help with brainstorming, generate different writing styles (poetry, scripts, email drafts), and even translate creative concepts into images or sounds.

Specific Functionalities

- **Search and Summarization:** Ask questions, request summaries of topics, compare and contrast, get detailed explanations of scientific principles, historical events, and more.
- **Writing and Translation:** Ask for help with drafting emails, reports, articles, or blog posts. It can translate languages, change the tone of written content, or turn your instructions into different creative formats.
- **Problem-solving:** Need help debugging code snippets? Provide step-by-step instructions or pose mathematical problems, and Gemini will try to work out the solutions.
- **Image/Visuals:** Get image descriptions, visual question-answering (ask questions about a provided image) and translate your ideas into visualizations (not as strong as dedicated image-generation models).
- **Conversation and Chat:** Gemini can maintain more engaging and informative conversations across a wider range of topics compared to earlier chatbots.

Limitations of Google Gemini 1.0

The limitations of Gemini 1.0 are listed below:

- **Imperfect Accuracy:** Like all AI models, there's always a potential for errors or omissions in the information provided. It's essential to keep a critical eye and fact-check important information.
- **Inability to Perform Real-World Actions:** Gemini can't perform actions in the physical world; it can't make a phone call, control physical devices, drive a car, and so on.
- **Lacks Sentience/Self-Awareness:** It's crucial to remember that Gemini is a sophisticated tool, not a sentient being.
- **Evolving Nature:** Gemini, like other LLM's, is constantly learning and fine-tuning, and its capabilities are likely to expand.

Important Reminder: It's vital to have realistic expectations while being open to Gemini's impressive abilities and exploring the different ways it can be used creatively and productively.

GEMINI ULTRA FEATURES THAT ARE NOT IN GEMINI PRO

The following prompt was supplied to Gemini Ultra regarding the features that are available in Gemini Ultra that are not available in Gemini Pro.

Prompt: Please provide a detailed description of the features in Gemini Ultra that are not available in Gemini Pro.

Ultra: While both Gemini Ultra and Gemini Pro are powerful language models, Gemini Ultra boasts advanced features in several areas that differentiate it from Gemini Pro. Here's a breakdown:

Key Features Exclusive to Gemini Ultra

Superior Multimodal Handling: Gemini Ultra truly excels in processing and understanding relationships between different modalities (text, images, video, audio). This is in contrast to Pro, which offers robust capabilities but without the same depth of multimodal reasoning that Ultra demonstrates.

Example: Ask a question like "Compare this painting to the song description I'm providing. What similarities in mood do you perceive?" Gemini Ultra might analyze the painting's composition and colors along with the song lyrics to find common emotional connections.

Complex Reasoning and Problem-Solving: Gemini Ultra excels in tasks requiring advanced logic, abstract thinking, and planning. These can include:

Mathematical Reasoning: Solving intricate mathematical problems, particularly those presented visually.

Planning: Outlining the steps required to achieve a given goal in a scenario.

Code Fluency: Gemini Ultra has unparalleled understanding and interaction with code:

Bug Identification: Spotting errors and suggesting corrections in code samples.

Code Translation: Converting code from one programming language to another.

Extended Memory and Context: Gemini Ultra operates with a larger memory footprint than Pro does. This allows it to effectively handle significantly longer documents, integrate information across complex dialogues, and maintain better context throughout conversations.

Things to Consider

Resource Intensity: The superior capabilities of Gemini Ultra come at the cost of increased computational requirements. Gemini Pro is often a more practical and efficient choice for many tasks.

Availability: Gemini Ultra is still primarily in the research phase. Public access is far more limited than it is for Gemini Pro.

In Summary

Gemini Ultra is meant for highly complex tasks that involve nuanced reasoning, understanding diverse input types, or deep knowledge about code. Its enhanced capabilities might be less critical for general language generation, straightforward summaries, or tasks that Gemini Pro already does exceptionally well.

Contact the author if you'd like more detailed examples of how these feature differences play out in practical scenarios.

How can I upload a CSV file in Google Gemini?

Gemini Ultra versus GPT-4: A Detailed Comparison

Feature	Gemini Ultra	GPT-4
Multimodality	Text, images, video, audio	Primarily text, some image capabilities
Code Interaction	Superior code understanding and capabilities	More limited code interaction
Document Handling	Higher document understanding scores (DOCVQA)	Strong, but Gemini Ultra holds an edge
Reasoning	Shows advantage in visual-context math problems	Highly capable, close competition
Customization	Less information on customization options	Offers customizable versions for specific tasks

Strengths of Gemini Ultra

Versatile Multimodal Skillset: Handling multiple input types makes it an adaptable problem-solver.

Coding Prowess: Its ability to interact with code is a powerful asset.

Handling of Complex Information: Excelling with dense documents makes it ideal for extracting specific insights.

Weaknesses of Gemini Ultra

Limited Public Access: Gemini Ultra isn't publicly available, hindering widespread testing and usage.

Potential for Bias: As with any LLM, the risk of harmful biases in responses remains a challenge.

Fact-Checking: Even powerful LLMs struggle with discerning objective truth, especially in nuanced, real-world scenarios.

Future Developments: Where Gemini Ultra Could Go

Enhanced Reasoning: Expect improvements in logical reasoning and problem-solving, extending beyond its current visual-mathematical advantages.

Real-World Integration: Gemini Ultra's abilities could be further integrated into Google products and services (e.g., advanced search capabilities, coding assistance, multimedia content analysis).

Open Access?: Potential future public access would spur innovation and exploration of its potential uses.

Important Considerations

It's vital to remember that the AI field is rapidly evolving. Benchmark comparisons can change quickly. Also, both Gemini Ultra and GPT-4 are incredibly powerful models; "better" can depend heavily on the specific task at hand.

An introduction to Gemini can be found here: *https://www.techrepublic.com/article/google-bard-cheat-sheet/*

Contact the author if you would like to dive deeper into a specific aspect of Gemini Ultra or have other questions.

UPLOADING CSV FILES IN GEMINI ULTRA

The following prompt was supplied to Gemini Ultra to explain how to upload CSV files.

```
Prompt: Please describe how to upload CSV files in Gemini
Ultra.

Ultra: While Google Gemini excels in many areas, it doesn't
have a built-in functionality for directly uploading and
processing CSV files. Here's why, along with alternative
approaches to work with your CSV data using the power of
Gemini:
```

Why You Can't Directly Upload to Gemini

Understanding versus. Processing: Gemini is a language model. It's superb at understanding language, generating text, and making connections between different types of information. CSV files are structured data tables that require additional tools or techniques to parse and understand their contents.

LLMs focus on natural language: Gemini is tailored for processing and interacting with the "messy" nature of human language rather than highly structured data formats like CSVs.

How to Make Gemini Work With Your CSV Data

Here are a few strategies:

1. External Preprocessing with Automation Tools

    Tools:

    Hexomatic (*https://hexomatic.com/automation/google-gemini*)

    Zapier ([<invalid URL removed>])

    Integromat ([<invalid URL removed>])

    Process:

    Use these platforms to read and parse your CSV file's contents.

    Extract relevant data points as text.

    Feed the extracted information to Gemini using these tool's automation abilities.

    Gemini can then work on summaries, questions, or generate insights based on this structured data now converted into plain text.

2. Coding Workarounds

    Programming Languages: Utilize Python or other scripting languages.

    Libraries: Employ libraries such as "pandas" to read the CSV file.

    Interact with Gemini:

    Send relevant text excerpts to Gemini through an API if such integration is available.

    Manually provide relevant textual summaries derived from your CSV for Gemini to process.

3. Hybrid Approach (If Gemini Access Allows)

    This requires some knowledge of prompting and depends on if the Gemini you have access to allows more "tool-like" functionality:

    Prompt Structure: Design prompts that guide Gemini on understanding the CSV structure (column names, data types).

    CSV Snippets: Feed in small text chunks of the CSV to Gemini within your prompts

    Gemini as Interpreter: Ask Gemini to analyze or answer questions about the snippet you provided

    Important note: The method and effectiveness of working with CSV data and Gemini will depend on the specific Gemini interface or API you have access to. Some versions might have increasing capability to understand tabular data or at least handle structured prompts in a flexible manner.

Let me know if you have a specific task in mind using a CSV file and Google Gemini, and I can try to suggest a more tailored approach!

GOOGLE GEMINI WITH CLOUD-RELATED GOOGLE PRODUCTS

Gemini has integration with a plethora of products. The following bullet list contains cloud-related products that are integrated with Google Gemini:

- Google Cloud
- Google AI Studio
- Google Vertex AI

The following prompt was supplied to Gemini Ultra to describe the role of Gemini in Google Cloud.

```
Prompt: Please provide a detailed description of the role
of Gemini in Google Cloud.

Ultra: Absolutely! Here's a detailed look at Gemini's
role within Google Cloud and its influence on the Android
ecosystem:
```

Gemini and Google Cloud

- **Vertex AI Integration:** Gemini is being integrated into Google Cloud's Vertex AI platform, which powers various machine learning services for developers and enterprises. Here's how this impacts Vertex AI:
  - **Improved Search Capabilities:** Gemini enhances search abilities within Vertex AI applications. Users can search for relevant datasets, models, and other resources more naturally and efficiently using everyday language rather than technical queries.
  - **Advanced Conversational AI:** Gemini-powered chatbots enable more dynamic and helpful interactions for users seeking support or interacting with AI agents within Vertex AI-powered apps.
  - **Code Generation and Understanding:** Gemini assists in generating code snippets based on instructions and can provide explanations of existing code for quicker development and troubleshooting.
- **Cloud API Enhancements:** The development of a dedicated Gemini API for Cloud products promises more intelligent functionality across several services:
  - **Smarter Recommendations:** Across services like Google Docs, Sheets, and other products, expect more context-aware suggestions, autocompletions, and better error correction leveraging Gemini's deep understanding.

• **Document and Data Analysis:** Analyzing datasets, reports, or other forms of content within Cloud Services would benefit from Gemini's ability to generate insightful summaries and answer in-depth questions about the data.

The Future

The influence of Gemini in both Google Cloud and Android highlights a trend toward simplifying user interaction with complex systems. This opens up the potential for smarter tools, increased accessibility, and ultimately more helpful AI woven into Google's services and devices.

SUMMARY

This chapter started with a discussion of generative AI, along with some of the major companies, such as Google, OpenAI, Cohere, and HuggingFace.

Following was information about prompt engineering, which addresses the various ways that you can design the content of the prompts that you provide to an LLM.

Next you learned about Google Gemini and the three models that are available, which are Ultra, Pro, and Nano. You also learned about Gemini 1.5 versus Gemini 1.0, and a comparison of Gemini Ultra with GPT-4.

Furthermore, was instruction about Gemini Ultra features that are not available in Gemini Pro, followed by a description of how to upload CSV files in Gemini Ultra. Finally, you learned about some cloud-related Google products that are integrated with Google Gemini.

2

PROMPT ENGINEERING

This chapter provides a fast-paced introduction to prompt engineering, with various types of prompts that you can use with many LLMs.

The first section of this chapter explains the difference between prompts and completions, as well as different types of prompts, such as instruction prompts, reverse prompts, and system prompts.

The second section in this chapter touches on prompts for different LLMs, as well as a list of poorly worded prompts, along with an explanation of why they are poorly worded.

The third section in this chapter describes aspects of LLM development, such as different "families" of LLMs that are based on whether they involve an encoder, a decoder, or both in the Transformer architecture. You will also learn about LLM size versus performance, emergent abilities of LLMs, and undertrained LLMs.

One other point to keep in mind: some of the sections in this chapter contain detailed information, so if you are new to LLMs, consider skimming through this chapter instead of trying to absorb everything (you can always return to this chapter later on).

WHAT IS PROMPT ENGINEERING?

You might have already heard about text generators, such as GPT-3, and DALL-E 2 from OpenAI, Jurassic from AI21, Midjourney from Midjourney Inc., and Stable Diffusion from Stability AI, which can perform text-to-image generation. *Prompt engineering* refers to devising text-based prompts that enable AI-based systems to improve the output that is generated. The result is that the output more closely matches whatever users want to produce from the AI. By way of analogy, think of prompts as similar to the role of coaches: they offer advice and suggestions to help people perform better in their given tasks.

Since prompts are based on words, the challenge involves learning how different words can affect the generated output. Moreover, it is difficult to predict how systems respond to a given prompt. For instance, if you want to generate a landscape, the difference between a dark landscape and a bright landscape is intuitive. However, if you want a beautiful landscape, how would an AI system generate a corresponding image? As you can surmise, "concrete" words are easier than abstract or subjective words for AI systems that generate images from text. Let us consider the previous example: how would you visualize the following?

- a beautiful landscape
- a beautiful song
- a beautiful movie

Although prompt engineering started with text-to-image generation, there are other types of prompt engineering, such as audio-based prompts that interpret emphasized text and emotions that are detected in speech, and sketch-based prompts that generate images from drawings. The most recent focus of attention involves text-based prompts for generating videos, which presents exciting opportunities for artists and designers. An example of image-to-image *processing* is accessible here:

https://huggingface.co/spaces/fffiloni/stable-diffusion-color-sketch

Prompts and Completions

A *prompt* is a text string that users provide to LLMs, and a *completion* is the text that users receive from LLMs. Prompts assist LLMs in completing a request (task), and they can vary in length. Although prompts can be any text string, including a random string, the quality and structure of prompts affects the quality of completions.

Think of prompts as a mechanism for giving "guidance" to LLMs, or even as a way to "coach" LLMs into providing desired answers. The number of tokens in a prompt plus the number of tokens in the completion can be at most 2,048 tokens.

Types of Prompts

The following list contains well-known types prompts for LLMs:

- zero-shot prompts
- one-shot prompts
- few-shot prompts
- instruction prompts

A *zero-shot prompt* contains a description of a task, whereas a *one-shot prompt* consists of a single example for completing a task. As you can probably surmise, *few-shot prompts* consist of multiple examples (typically between ten and one hundred). In all cases, a clear description of the task or tasks is recommended: more tasks provide GPT-3 with more information, which in turn can lead to more accurate completions.

T0 (for "zero shot") is an interesting LLM: although T0 is 16 times smaller (11 GB) than GPT-3 (175 GB), T0 has outperformed GPT-3 on language-related tasks. T0 can perform well on unseen NLP tasks (i.e., tasks that are new to T0) because it was trained on a dataset containing multiple tasks.

The following Web page provides the Github repository for T0, a site for training T0 directly in a browser, as well as more details about T0 and a 3GB version of T0:

https://github.com/bigscience-workshop/t-zero

As you can probably surmise, T0++ is based on T0, and it was trained with extra tasks beyond the set of tasks on which T0 was trained.

Another important detail is the first three prompts in the preceding list are also called zero-shot learning, one-shot learning, and few-shot learning, respectively.

Instruction Prompts

Instruction prompts are used for fine tuning LLMs, and they specify a format (determined by you) for the manner in which the LLM is expected to conform in its responses. You can prepare your own instruction prompts or you can access prompt template libraries that contain different templates for different tasks, along with different datasets. Various prompt instruction templates are publicly available, such as the following links that provides prompt templates (see subsequent section for an example) for Llama:

https://github.com/devbrones/llama-prompts

https://pub.towardsai.net/llama-gpt4all-simplified-local-chatgpt-ab7d28d34923

Reverse Prompts

Another technique uses a reverse order: input prompts are answers and the response are the questions associated with the answers (similar to a popular game show). For example, given a French sentence, you might ask the model, "What English text might have resulted in this French translation?"

System Prompts Versus Agent Prompts

The distinction between a system prompt and an agent prompt often comes up in the context of conversational AI systems and chatbot design.

A *system prompt* is typically an initial message or cue given by the system to guide the user on what they can do or to set expectations about the interaction.

It often serves as an introduction or a way to guide users on how to proceed. Here are several examples of system prompts:

- "Welcome to ChatBotX! You can ask me questions about weather, news, or sports. How can I assist you today?"
- "Hello! For account details, press 1. For technical support, press 2."
- "Greetings! Type 'order' to track your package or 'help' for assistance."

By contrast, an *agent prompt* is a message generated by the AI model or agent in response to a user's input during the course of an interaction. It is a part of the back-and-forth exchange within the conversation. The agent prompt guides the user to provide more information, clarifies ambiguity, or nudges the user toward a specific action. Here are some examples of agent prompts:

```
User: "I'm looking for shoes."
Agent Prompt: "Great! Are you looking for men's or women's
shoes?"
User: "I can't log in."
Agent Prompt: "I'm sorry to hear that. Can you specify if
you are having trouble with your password or username?"
User: "Tell me a joke."
Agent Prompt: "Why did the chicken join a band? Because it
had the drumsticks!"
```

The fundamental difference between the two is their purpose and placement in the interaction. A system prompt is often at the beginning of an interaction, setting the stage for the conversation. An agent prompt occurs during the conversation, steering the direction of the dialogue based on user input.

Both types of prompts are crucial for creating a fluid and intuitive conversational experience for users. They guide the user and help ensure that the system understands and addresses the user's needs effectively.

Prompt Templates

Prompt templates are predefined formats or structures used to instruct a model or system to perform a specific task. They serve as a foundation for generating prompts, where certain parts of the template can be filled in or customized to produce a variety of specific prompts. By way of analogy, prompt templates are the counterpart to macros that you can define in some text editors.

Prompt templates are especially useful when working with language models, as they provide a consistent way to query the model across multiple tasks or data points. In particular, prompt templates can make it easier to:

- ensure consistency when querying a model multiple times
- facilitate batch processing or automation.
- reduce errors and variations in how questions are posed to the model

As an example, suppose you are working with an LLM and you want to translate English sentences into French. An associated prompt template could be the following:

"Translate the following English sentence into French: {sentence}"

Note that {sentence} is a placeholder that you can replace with any English sentence.

You can use the preceding prompt template to generate specific prompts:

- "Translate the following English sentence into French: 'Hello, how are you?'"
- "Translate the following English sentence into French: 'I love ice cream.'"

As you can see, prompt templates enable you to easily generate a variety of prompts for different sentences without having to rewrite the entire instruction each time. In fact, this concept can be extended to more complex tasks and can incorporate multiple placeholders or more intricate structures, depending on the application.

Prompts for Different LLMs

GPT-3, ChatGPT, and GPT-4 are LLMs that are all based on the transformer architecture and are fundamentally similar in their underlying mechanics. ChatGPT is essentially a version of the GPT model fine-tuned specifically for conversational interactions. GPT-4 is an evolution or improvement over GPT-3 in terms of scale and capabilities.

The differences in prompts for these models mainly arise from the specific use case and context, rather than inherent differences between the models. Here are some prompting differences that are based on use cases.

GPT-3 can be used for a wide range of tasks beyond just conversation, from content generation to code writing. Here are two examples of prompts for GPT-3:

- "Translate the following English text to French: 'Hello, how are you?'"
- "Write a Python function that calculates the factorial of a number."

ChatGPT is specifically fine-tuned for conversational interactions. Here are examples of prompts for two different conversations with ChatGPT:

- User: "Can you help me with my homework?"
  ChatGPT: "Of course! What subject or topic do you need help with?"
- User: "'Tell me a joke."
- ChatGPT: "Why did the chicken cross the playground? To get to the other slide!"

GPT-4 provides a larger scale and refinements, so the prompts would be similar in nature to GPT-3 but might yield more accurate or nuanced outputs. Here are two examples of prompts for GPT-4:

- "Provide a detailed analysis of quantum mechanics in relation to general relativity."
- "Generate a short story based on a post-apocalyptic world with a theme of hope."

These three models accept natural language prompts and produce natural language outputs. The fundamental way you interact with them remains consistent.

The main difference comes from the context in which the model is being used and any fine tuning that has been applied. ChatGPT, for instance, is designed to be more conversational, so while you can use GPT-3 for chats, ChatGPT might produce more contextually relevant conversational outputs.

When directly interacting with these models, especially through an API, you might also have control over parameters like "temperature" (controlling randomness) and "max tokens" (controlling response length). Adjusting these can shape the responses, regardless of which GPT variant you are using.

In essence, while the underlying models have differences in scale and specific training/fine tuning, the way you prompt them remains largely consistent: clear, specific natural language prompts yield the best results.

Poorly-Worded Prompts

When crafting prompts, be as clear and specific as possible to guide the response in the desired direction. Ambiguous or vague prompts can lead to a wide range of responses, many of which might not be useful or relevant to the user's actual intent.

Poorly worded prompts are often vague, ambiguous, or too broad, and they can lead to confusion, misunderstanding, or nonspecific responses from AI models. Here are some examples of poorly worded prompts, along with explanations:

"Tell me about that thing."
Problem: Too vague. What "thing" is being referred to?

"Why did it happen?"
Problem: No context. What event or situation is being discussed?

"Explain stuff."
Problem: Too broad. What specific "stuff" should be explained?

"Do what is needful."
Problem: Ambiguous. What specific action is required?

"I want information."
Problem: Not specific enough. What type of information is desired?

"Can you get me the thing from the place?"
Problem: Both "thing" and "place" are unclear.

"Where can I buy what's-his-name's book?"
Problem: Ambiguous reference. Who is "what's-his-name ?"

"How do you do the process?"
Problem: Which "process" is being referred to?

"Describe the importance of the topic."
Problem: The "topic" is not specified.

"Why is it bad or good?"
Problem: No context. What is "it?"

"Help with the issue."
Problem: Vague. What specific issue requires assistance?

"Things to consider for the task."
Problem: Ambiguous. What "task" is being discussed?

"How does this work?"
Problem: Lack of specificity. What is "this?"

THE GPT-3 PLAYGROUND

OpenAI provides the GPT-3 Playground, which is a Web-based tool for entering prompts in a text field and receiving completions from GPT-3. The Playground supports most of the functionality that is available directly through the GPT-3 API.

Moreover, the Playground enables you to interact with GPT-3 without writing any code. In essence, the OpenAI Playground enables you to easily use

GPT-3 to train the engine to produce text output. The GPT-3 Playground also provides a set of saved prompts that are called "presets."

The first step is to navigate to the GPT-3 Playground via this link where you will be prompted to sign into your account:

https://gpt3demo.com/apps/openai-gpt-3-playground

The screen in the preceding link displays three sections: a "Get Started" section, a "Playground" section, and third section that consists of a drop-down list and sliders for tunable parameters.

The middle section is the input text for GPT-3, which has two parts: 1) a start sequence that is the text string `Text:`, followed by one or more text blocks (provided by you) that provides GPT-3 with sample output text. The second paragraph contains the same string `Text:` that indicates the end of your input text.

Now let's turn our attention to inference parameters, which is the topic of the next section.

INFERENCE PARAMETERS

After you have completed the fine-tuning step for an LLM, you are in a position to set values for various so-called inference parameters. The GPT-3 API supports numerous inference parameters, which are shown in the following bulleted list:

* `engine`
* `prompt`
* `max_tokens`
* `top_p`
* `top_k`
* `frequency_penalty`
* `presence_penalty`
* `token length`
* `stop tokens`
* `temperature`

The `engine` inference parameter can be one of the four GPT-3 models, such as `text-ada-001`. The `prompt` parameter is simply the input text that you provide. The `presence_penalty` inference parameter enables more relevant responses when you specify higher values for this parameter.

The `max_tokens` inference parameter specifies the maximum number of tokens: sample values are 100, 200, or 256. The `top_p` inference parameter can be a positive integer that specifies the top-most results to select. The `frequency_penalty` is an inference parameter that pertains to the frequency of repeated words. A smaller value for this parameter increases the number of repeated words.

The "token length" parameter specifies the total number of words that are in the input sequence that is processed by the LLM (not the maximum length of each token).

The "stop tokens" parameter controls the length of the generated output of an LLM. If this parameter equals 1, then only a single sentence is generated, whereas a value of 2 indicates that the generated output is limited to one paragraph.

The "top k" parameter specifies the number of tokens—which is the value for k—that are chosen, with the constraint that the chosen tokens have the highest probabilities. For example, if "top k" is equal to 3, then only the 3 tokens with the highest probabilities are selected.

The "top p" parameter is a floating point number between 0.0 and 1.0, and it's the upper bound on the sum of the probabilities of the chosen tokens. For example, if a discrete probability distribution consists of the set S = {0.1, 0.2, 0.3, 0.4} and the value of the "top p" parameter is 0.3, then only the tokens with associated probabilities of 0.1 and 0.2 can be selected.

Thus, the "top k" and the "top p" parameters provide two mechanisms for limiting the number of tokens that can be selected.

Temperature Parameter

The temperature hyper parameter is a floating point number between 0 and 1 inclusive, and its default value is 0.7. One interesting value for the temperature is 0.8: this will result in GPT-3 selecting a next token that does *not* have the maximum probability.

The "temperature" parameter T is a nonnegative floating point number whose value influences the extent to which the model uses randomness. Specifically, smaller values for the temperature parameter that are closer to 0 involve less randomness (i.e., more deterministic), whereas larger values for the temperature parameter involve more randomness.

The temperature parameter T is directly associated with the softmax function that is applied during the final step in the transformer architecture. The value of T alters the formula for the softmax function, as described later in this section. A key point to remember is that selecting tokens based on a softmax function means that the selected token is the token with the highest probability.

By contrast, larger values for the parameter T enable randomness in the choice of the next token, which means that a token can be selected even though its associated probability is less than the maximum probability. While this might seem counter-intuitive, it turns out that some values of T (such as 0.8) result in output text that is more natural sounding, from a human's perspective, than the output text in which tokens are selected if they have the maximum probability. Finally, a temperature value of 1 is the same as the standard softmax () function.

Temperature and the softmax() Function

The temperature parameter T appears in the *denominator* of the exponent of the Euler constant e in the softmax function. Thus, instead of the softmax numerators of the form $e^{(x_i)}$, the modified softmax function contains numerator terms of the form $e^{(x_i/T)}$, where $\{x_1, x_2, \ldots, x_n\}$ comprise a set of numbers that form a discrete probability distribution (explained in the next section).

As a reminder, the denominator of each term generated by the softmax function consists of the sum of the terms in the set $\{e^{(x_1)}, e^{(x_2)}, \ldots, e^{(x_n)}\}$. However, the denominator of the terms involving the temperature parameter T is slightly different: it's the sum of the terms in the set $\{e^{(x_1/T)}, e^{(x_2/T)}, \ldots, e^{(x_n/T)}\}$.

Interestingly, the softmax function with the temperature parameter T is the same as the Boltzmann distribution that is described here:

https://en.wikipedia.org/wiki/Boltzmann_distribution

The following `Python` code snippet provides an example of specifying values for various hyper parameters, which include specifies a GPT-3 engine:

```
response = openai.Completion.create(
  engine="text-ada-001",
  prompt="",
  temperature=0.7,
  max_tokens=256,
  top_p=1,
  frequency_penalty=0,
  presence_penalty=0
)
```

Navigate to the following URL for more information regarding inference parameters in GPT-3: *https://huggingface.co/blog/inference-endpoints-llm*

ASPECTS OF LLM DEVELOPMENT

Modern LLMs use one of three variants of the transformer architecture: encoder-only LLMs, decoder-only LLMs, and LLMs that are based on an encoder as well as a decoder (which is actually the original transformer architecture).

For your convenience, this section provides a list of language models that belong to each of these three types of models.

With the preceding points in mind, some of the better-known encoder-based LLMs include the following:

- AlBERT
- BERT
- DistilBERT

- ELECTRA
- RoBERTa

The preceding LLMs are well-suited for performing NLP tasks such as NER and extractive question-answering tasks. In addition to encoder-only LLMs, there are several well-known decoder-based LLMs that include the following:

- CTRL
- GPT/GPT-2
- Transformer XK

The preceding LLMs perform text *generation*, whereas encoder-only models perform next word *prediction*. Finally, some of the well-known encoder/decoder-based LLMs include the following:

- BART
- mBART
- Marian
- T5

The preceding LLMs perform summarization, translation, and generate question-answering.

One trend involves the use of fine tuning, zero/one/few-shot training, and prompt-based learning with respect to LLMs. Fine tuning is typically accompanied by a fine-tuning dataset, and if the latter is not available (or infeasible), few-shot training might be an acceptable alternative.

One outcome from training the Jurassic-1 LLM is that wider and shallower is better than narrower and deeper with respect to performance because a wider context allows for more calculations to be performed in parallel.

Another result from Chinchilla is that smaller models that are trained on a corpus with a very large number of tokens can be more performant than larger models that are trained on a more modest number of tokens.

The success of the GlaM and Switch LLMs (both from Google) suggests that sparse transformers, in conjunction with MoE (mixture of experts), is also an interesting direction, potentially leading to even better results in the future.

In addition, there is the possibility of the "over curation" of data, which is to say that performing *very* detailed data curation to remove spurious-looking tokens does not guarantee that models will produce better results on those curated datasets.

The use of prompts has revealed an interesting detail: the results of similar yet different prompts can lead to substantively different responses. Thus, the goal is to create well-crafted prompts, which are inexpensive and yet can be a somewhat elusive task.

Another area of development pertains to the continued need for benchmarks that leverage better and more complex datasets, especially when

LLMs exceed human performance. Specifically, a benchmark becomes out-dated when all modern LLMs can pass the suite of tests in that benchmark. Two such benchmarks are XNLI and BigBench ("Beyond the Imitation Game Benchmark").

The following Web page provides a fairly extensive list of general NLP benchmarks as well as language-specific NLP benchmarks:

https://mr-nlp.github.io/posts/2021/05/benchmarks-in-nlp/

The following Web page provides a list of monolingual transformer-based pre-trained language models:

https://mr-nlp.github.io/posts/2021/05/tptlms-list/

LLM Size Versus Performance

Let us consider the size-versus-performance question: although larger models such as GPT-3 can perform better than smaller models, it is not always the case. In particular, models that are variants of GPT-3 have mixed results: some smaller variants perform almost as well as GPT-3, and some larger models perform only marginally better than GPT-3.

A recent trend involves developing models that are based on the decoder component of the transformer architecture. Such models are frequently meas-ured by their performance via zero-shot, one-shot, and few-shot training in comparison to other LLMs. This trend, as well as the development of ever-larger LLMs, is likely to continue for the foreseeable future.

Interestingly, decoder-only LLMs can perform tasks such as token predic-tion, and can slightly out-perform encoder-only models on benchmarks such as SuperGLUE. However, such decoder-based models tend to be significantly larger than encoder-based models, and the latter tend to be more efficient than the former.

Hardware is another consideration in terms of optimizing model perfor-mance, which can incur a greater cost, and hence might be limited to only a handful of companies. Due to the high cost of hardware, another initiative involves training LLMs on the Jean Zay supercomputer in France:

https://venturebeat.com/2022/01/10/inside-bigscience-the-quest-to-build-a-powerful-open-language-model/

Emergent Abilities of LLMs

The *emergent abilities* of LLMs refers to abilities that are present in larger models that do not exist in smaller models. In simplified terms, as models increase in size, there is a discontinuous "jump"" whereby abilities manifest themselves in a larger model with no apparent or clear-cut reason.

The interesting aspect of emergent abilities is the possibility of expanding capabilities of language models through additional scaling. More detailed information is accessible in the Wei et al. (2022) research paper "Emergent Abilities of Large Language Models" that can be accessed here: *https://arxiv. org/abs/2206.07682*

In his essay "More Is Different" Nobel-Prize-winning physicist Philip Anderson stated, "Emergence is when quantitative changes in a system result in qualitative changes in behavior" (Anderson, 1972).

Interestingly, Wei et al. (2022) describes a scenario in which few-shot prompting is considered emergent: "The ability to perform a task via few-shot prompting is emergent when a model has random performance until a certain scale, after which performance increases to well-above random" (p. 3). (Be sure to examine Table 1 in the Wei et al. paper, which provides details regarding "few-shot prompting abilities" (e.g., truthfulness, the MMLU Benchmark) as well as "augmented prompting abilities" (e.g., chain of thought and instruction following).)

Note that emergent abilities *cannot* be predicted by extrapolation of the behavior of smaller models because (by definition) emergent abilities are not present in smaller models. No doubt there will be more research that explores the extent to which further model scaling can lead to more emergent abilities in LLMs.

KAPLAN AND UNDERTRAINED MODELS

Kaplan et al. (2020) provided (empirical) power laws regarding the performance of language models, which they assert depends on the following:

* model size
* dataset size
* amount of compute for training

Kaplan et al. asserted that changing the network width or depth have minimal effects. They also claimed that optimal training of very large models involves a relatively modest amount of data. The paper with the relevant details is accessible online:

https://arxiv.org/abs/2001.08361

However, Chinchilla is a 70 B LLM that was trained on a dataset that is much larger than the size that is recommended by Kaplan et al. In fact, Chinchilla achieved SOTA status has surpassed the performance of the following LLMs, all of which are between two and seven times larger than Chinchilla:

* Gopher (280B)
* GPT-3 (175B)
* J1-Jumbo (178B)
* LaMDA (137B)
* MT-NLG (530B)

In addition, the creators of the Chinchilla LLM wrote the paper "Scaling Laws for Neural Language Models," which includes the suggested number of tokens for various models sizes to be fully trained instead of under trained (see Table 3 in that document). For example, the suggested training set sizes for models that have 175 B, 520 B, and 1 trillion parameters is 3.7 trillion tokens, 11.0 trillion tokens, and 21.2 trillion tokens, respectively. The largest entry in the same table is LMMs with 10 trillion parameters, with a recommended training set size of 216.2 trillion parameters.

Obviously, an LLM that exceeds 1 trillion parameters faces a significant challenge creating datasets of the recommended size, as described in the paper from the authors of Chinchilla. One interesting possibility involves ASR (briefly discussed in Chapter 4), which might enable the generation of datasets that are larger than 10 trillion tokens by transcribing audio to text. Indeed, some speculation suggests that GPT-4 might leverage ASR to create such a dataset.

SUMMARY

This chapter started with a description of prompt engineering, which involves various techniques, such as instruction prompts, reverse prompts, system prompts, CoT, and various other techniques. In addition, you saw examples of poorly worded prompts, followed by details about the GPT-3 Playground.

Finally, you learned about various GPT-based LLMs, as well as information about aspects of LLM development, such as LLM size versus performance, emergent abilities of LLMs, and under-trained models.

3

INTRODUCTION TO CSS3

C hapter 3 is the first of three chapters that discusses CSS3, with a focus on CSS3 features that enable you to create vivid graphics effects. Keep in mind that this chapter, as well as Chapter 4, contain manually crafted CSS3 code samples, whereas Chapter 5 contains CSS3 code samples that were generated by Google Gemini.

The first section of this chapter contains a short section that discusses the structure of a minimal HTML document, followed by a brief discussion regarding browser support for CSS3 and online tools that can be helpful in this regard. CSS3 style sheets are referenced in HTML pages; therefore, it's important to understand the limitations that exist with respect to browser support for CSS3.

The second section of this chapter contains various code samples that illustrate how to create shadow effects, how to render rectangles with rounded corners, and also how to use linear and radial gradients. The third section of this chapter covers CSS3 transforms (scale, rotate, skew, and translate), along with code samples that illustrate how to apply transforms to HTML elements and to PNG files.

When you have completed this chapter, you will know how to use the CSS3 methods translate(), rotate(), skew(), and scale(). Before you read this chapter, please keep in mind the following points. First, the CSS3 code samples in this book are for WebKit-based browsers, so the code will work on Microsoft® Windows®, Macintosh®, and Linux®.

Second, several chapters mention performing an Internet search to obtain more information about a specific topic. The rationale for doing so is that the relevance of online information depends on the knowledge level of the reader, so it's virtually impossible to find a one-size-fits-all link that is suitable for everyone's needs. Furthermore, topics that are less relevant to the theme or beyond the scope of this book will be covered more lightly, thereby maintaining a reasonable balance between the number of topics and the depth of explanation of the relevant details. With these points in mind, please be assured that referring you to the Internet is never intended to be "user unfriendly" in any manner.

Third, virtually all of the links in this book refer to open source projects, but you can also find very good commercial products; the choice of tools depends on the features that they support, the requirements for your project, and the size of your budget.[1]

HTML AND <DOCTYPE>

In addition to introducing many new semantic tags, HTML has simplified the <DOCTYPE> declaration for Web pages. This book does not contain a discussion of new HTML tags, but the HTML pages in this book do use the HTML <DOCTYPE> declaration. The typical structure of the HTML pages in this book looks like this:

```
<!DOCTYPE html>
<html lang="en">
<head>
 ...
</head>

<body>
 <div id="outer">
 ...
 </div>
</body>
</html>
```

Most of the "action" in the CSS3-based code samples takes place in the CSS3 selectors. As you will see later, code that involves JavaScript for rendering 2D shapes in an HTML Web page (such as HTML Canvas code) is embedded in a <script> element.

CSS3 FEATURES AND BROWSER SUPPORT

There are two important details about defining CSS3-based selectors for HTML pages. First, different browsers (and different browser versions) support different CSS3 features. One of the best Web sites for finding this detailed level of information is here: *http://caniuse.com/*. This Web site contains tabular information regarding CSS3 support in Internet Explorer® (IE), Firefox®, Safari®, Chrome™, and Opera™ browsers.

The second detail is that some CSS3 properties require browser-specific prefixes in order for them to work correctly, which is answered by GPT4 in the next section.

Browser-Specific Prefixes for CSS3

The following prompt was supplied to GPT4 in order to obtain information regarding vendor-specific prefixes for CSS3 in HTML Web pages.

```
Prompt:
Are vendor-specific prefixes required for CSS3 necessary
for HTML web pages?

ChatGPT:
As of my last update in April 2023, the necessity of using
vendor-specific prefixes in CSS3 for HTML Web pages depends
on several factors, including the specific CSS features you
are using, the range of browsers and their versions you aim
to support, and the rate at which these browsers adopt new
CSS features.

Vendor-specific prefixes are used to implement experimental
or nonstandardized features in web browsers. Common
prefixes include:
```

- `-webkit-` for Chrome, Safari, newer versions of Opera, and almost all iOS browsers
- `-moz-` for Firefox
- `-o-` for older versions of Opera
- `-ms-` for Internet Explorer and Microsoft Edge

Current State and Considerations:

1. **Improved Standardization**: Modern Web browsers have significantly improved in terms of standards compliance. Many CSS3 features that once required prefixes are now part of the standardized CSS3 specifications and are implemented uniformly across major browsers.

2. **Automatic Prefixing Tools**: Tools like Autoprefixer can be used in the development process. They automatically add necessary prefixes based on the project's browser support requirements. This has greatly simplified the process, reducing the need for manual prefixing.

3. **Feature Detection Over Browser Detection**: Modern best practices often recommend using feature detection (for instance, using Modernizr) instead of browser detection. This approach applies styles or fallbacks based on whether the browser supports a particular feature, rather than on which browser it is.

4. **Browser Update Frequency**: Browsers update frequently, meaning that more users are likely to be on versions that support standard CSS3 features. This reduces the need for vendor-specific prefixes for users on the latest versions.

5. **Fallbacks for Older Browsers**: If your audience includes users on older browsers that require these prefixes for certain features, then including

them is necessary. It's important to know your audience and their typical browser usage.

6. **Use of "Can I Use"**: Checking compatibility tables on Web sites like "Can I Use" is helpful. It provides current data on the support of various CSS features across different browsers and versions, indicating whether prefixes are needed.

In summary, while vendor-specific prefixes are not as widely required as they once were due to the increased standardization and frequent updates of browsers, they may still be necessary in certain situations, particularly when targeting older browsers or using very new, experimental features. Tools like Autoprefixer and strategies like feature detection are recommended to manage browser compatibility effectively.

As an illustration, the following code block shows examples of vendor-specific prefixes:

- `-ie-webkit-border-radius: 8px;`
- `-moz-webkit-border-radius: 8px;`
- `-o-webkit-border-radius: 8px;`
- `border-radius: 8px;`

In your CSS selectors, specify the attributes with browser-specific prefixes before the "generic" attribute, which serves as a default choice in the event that the browser-specific attributes are not selected. The CSS3 code samples in this book contain Webkit-specific prefixes, which helps us keep the CSS style sheets manageable in terms of size. If you need CSS style sheets that work on multiple browsers, there are essentially two options available. One option involves manually adding the CSS3 code with all the required browser-specific prefixes, which can be tedious to maintain and is also error prone. Another option is to use CSS frameworks (discussed in Chapter 2) that can programmatically generate the CSS3 code that contains all browser-specific prefixes.

A QUICK OVERVIEW OF CSS3 FEATURES

CSS3 adopts a modularized approach for extending existing CSS2 functionality as well as supporting new functionality. As such, CSS3 can be logically divided into the following categories:

- backgrounds/borders
- color
- media queries
- multicolumn layout
- selectors

With CSS3 you can create boxes with rounded corners and shadow effects; create rich graphics effects using linear and radial gradients; switch between portrait and landscape mode and detect the type of mobile device using media query selectors; produce multicolumn text rendering and formatting; and specify sophisticated node selection rules in selectors using first-child, last-child, first-of-type, and last-of-type.

CSS3 SHADOW EFFECTS AND ROUNDED CORNERS

CSS3 shadow effects are useful for creating vivid visual effects with simple selectors. You can use shadow effects for text as well as rectangular regions. CSS3 also enables you to easily render rectangles with rounded corners, so you do not need PNG files in order to create this effect.

CSS3 and Text-Shadow Effects

A shadow effect for text can make a Web page look more vivid and appealing. Listing 3.1 displays the contents of the HTML page TextShadow1.html, illustrating how to render text with a shadow effect, and Listing 3.2 displays the contents of the CSS style sheet TextShadow1.css that is referenced in Listing 3.1.

LISTING 3.1 TextShadow1.html

```
<!DOCTYPE html>
<html lang="en">
<head>
  <title>CSS Text Shadow Example</title>
  <meta charset="utf-8" />
  <link href="TextShadow1.css" rel="stylesheet"
                                type="text/css">
</head>

<body>
  <div id="text1">
    Line One Shadow Effect
  </div>
  <div id="text2">
    Line Two Shadow Effect
  </div>
  <div id="text3">
    Line Three Vivid Effect
  </div>

  <div id="text4">
    <span id="dd">13</span>
    <span id="mm">August</span>
    <span id="yy">2024</span>
  </div>
```

```
<div id="text5">
  <span id="dd">13</span>
  <span id="mm">August</span>
  <span id="yy">2024</span>
</div>

<div id="text6">
  <span id="dd">13</span>
  <span id="mm">August</span>
  <span id="yy">2024</span>
</div>
</body>
</html>
```

The code in Listing 3.1 is straightforward: there is a reference to the CSS style sheet `TextShadow1.css` that contains two CSS selectors. One selector specifies how to render the HTML `<div>` element whose `id` attribute has value `text1`, and the other selector is applied to the HTML `<div>` element whose `id` attribute is `text2`. The CSS3 `rotate()` function is included in this example; however, a more detailed discussion of this function is included later in this chapter.

LISTING 3.2 `TextShadow1.css`

```
#text1 {
  font-size: 24pt;
  text-shadow: 2px 4px 5px #00f;
}

#text2 {
  font-size: 32pt;
  text-shadow: 0px 1px 6px #000,
               4px 5px 6px #f00;
}

#text3 {
  font-size: 40pt;
  text-shadow: 0px 1px 6px   #fff,
               2px 4px 4px   #0ff,
               4px 5px 6px   #00f,
               0px 0px 10px #444,
               0px 0px 20px #844,
               0px 0px 30px #a44,
               0px 0px 40px #f44;
}

#text4 {
  position: absolute;
  top: 200px;
```

```
      right: 200px;
      font-size: 48pt;
      text-shadow: 0px 1px 6px    #fff,
                   2px 4px 4px    #0ff,
                   4px 5px 6px    #00f,
                   0px 0px 10px   #000,
                   0px 0px 20px   #448,
                   0px 0px 30px   #a4a,
                   0px 0px 40px   #fff;
      -webkit-transform: rotate(-90deg);
}

#text5 {
      position: absolute;
      left: 0px;
      font-size: 48pt;
      text-shadow: 2px 4px 5px #00f;
      -webkit-transform: rotate(-10deg);
}

#text6 {
      float: left;
      font-size: 48pt;
      text-shadow: 2px 4px 5px #f00;
      -webkit-transform: rotate(-170deg);
}

/* 'transform' is explained later */
#text1:hover, #text2:hover, #text3:hover,
#text4:hover, #text5:hover, #text6:hover {
-webkit-transform : scale(2) rotate(-45deg);
-transform : scale(2) rotate(-45deg);
}
```

The first selector in Listing 3.2 specifies a font-size of 24 and a text-shadow that renders text with a blue background (represented by the hexadecimal value #00f). The attribute text-shadow specifies (from left to right) the x-coordinate, the y-coordinate, the blur radius, and the color of the shadow. The second selector specifies a font-size of 32 and a red shadow background (#f00). The third selector creates a richer visual effect by specifying multiple components in the text-shadow property, chosen by experimenting with effects that are possible with different values in the various components.

The final CSS3 selector creates an animation effect when users hover over any of the six text strings; the details of the animation will be deferred until later in this chapter. Figure 3.1 displays the result of applying the CSS style sheet TextShadow1.css to the HTML <div> elements in the HTML page TextShadow1.html.

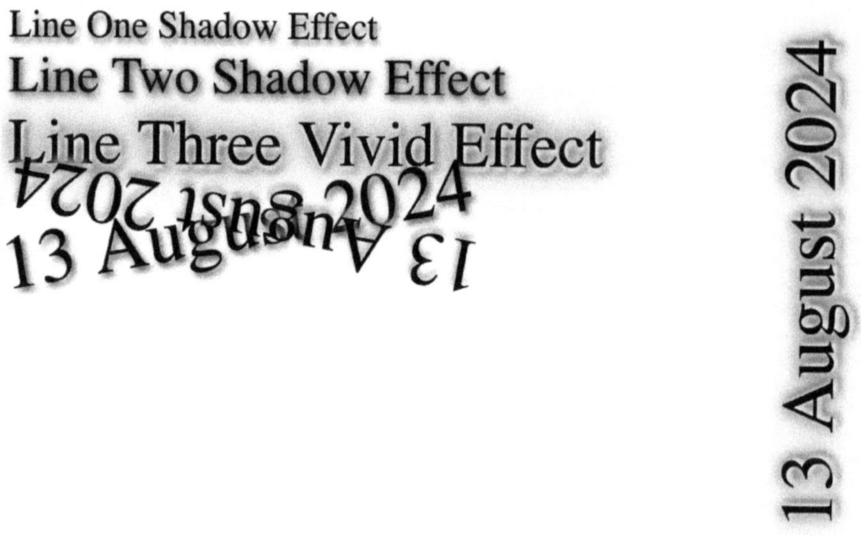

Line One Shadow Effect

Line Two Shadow Effect

Line Three Vivid Effect

13 August 2024

FIGURE 3.1 CSS3 text-shadow effects.

CSS3 and Box-Shadow Effects

You can also apply a shadow effect to a box that encloses a text string, which can be effective in terms of drawing attention to specific parts of a Web page. The same caveat regarding overuse applies to box shadows. Listing 3.3 displays the contents of the HTML page `BoxShadow1.html` that renders a box-shadow effect and Listing 3.4 displays the contents of `BoxShadow1.css` that contains the associated CSS3 selectors.

LISTING 3.3 `BoxShadow1.html`

```
<!DOCTYPE html>
<html lang="en">
<head>
  <title>CSS Box Shadow Example</title>
  <meta charset="utf-8" />
  <link href="BoxShadow1.css" rel="stylesheet"
                                 type="text/css">
</head>

<body>
  <div id="box1"> Line One with a Box Effect </div>
  <div id="box2"> Line Two with a Box Effect </div>
  <div id="box3"> Line Three with a Box Effect </div>
</body>
</html>
```

The code in Listing 3.3 references the CSS style sheet BoxShadow1.css (instead of TextShadow1.css) that contains three CSS selectors. These selectors specify how to render the HTML <div> elements whose id attribute has value box1, box2, and box3, respectively (and all three <div> elements are defined in BoxShadow1.html).

LISTING 3.4 BoxShadow1.css

```
#box1 {
  position:relative;top:10px;
  width: 50%;
  height: 30px;
  font-size: 20px;
  -moz-box-shadow: 10px 10px 5px #800;
  -webkit-box-shadow: 10px 10px 5px #800;
  box-shadow: 10px 10px 5px #800;
}

#box2 {
  position:relative;top:20px;
  width: 80%;
  height: 50px;
  font-size: 36px;
  padding: 10px;
  -moz-box-shadow: 14px 14px 8px #008;
  -webkit-box-shadow: 14px 14px 8px #008;
  box-shadow: 14px 14px 8px #008;
}

#box3 {
  position:relative;top:30px;
  width: 80%;
  height: 60px;
  font-size: 52px;
  padding: 10px;
  -moz-box-shadow: 14px 14px 8px #008;
  -webkit-box-shadow: 14px 14px 8px #008;
  box-shadow: 14px 14px 8px #008;
}
```

The first selector in Listing 3.4 specifies the attributes width, height, and font-size, which control the dimensions of the associated HTML <div> element and also the enclosed text string. The next three attributes consist of a Mozilla-specific box-shadow attribute, followed by a WebKit-specific box-shadow property, and finally the "generic" box-shadow attribute. Figure 3.2 displays the result of applying the CSS style sheet BoxShadow1.css to the HTML page BoxShadow1.html.

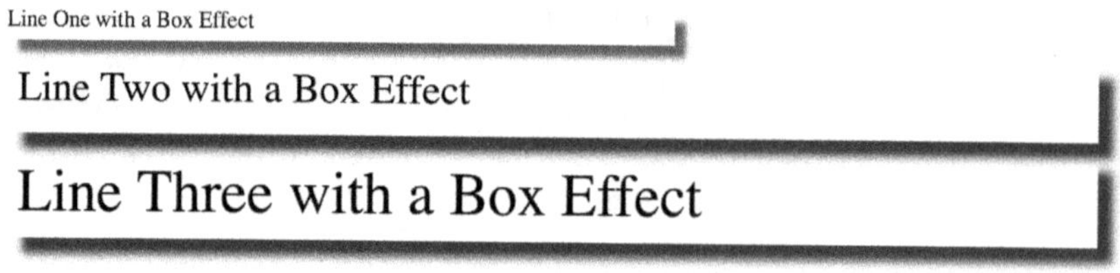

Line One with a Box Effect

Line Two with a Box Effect

Line Three with a Box Effect

FIGURE 3.2 CSS3 box-shadow effect.

CSS3 and Rounded Corners

Web developers have waited a long time for rounded corners in CSS, and CSS3 makes it very easy to render boxes with rounded corners. Listing 3.5 displays the contents of the HTML page `RoundedCorners1.html` that renders text strings in boxes with rounded corners, and Listing 3.6 displays the CSS file `RoundedCorners1.css`.

LISTING 3.5 `RoundedCorners1.html`

```
<!DOCTYPE html>
<html lang="en">
<head>
  <title>CSS Text Shadow Example</title>
  <meta charset="utf-8" />
  <link href="RoundedCorners1.css" rel="stylesheet"
                                  type="text/css">
</head>

<body>
  <div id="outer">
    <a href="#" class="anchor">Text Inside a Rounded
                                Rectangle</a>
  </div>

  <div id="text1">
    Line One of Text with a Shadow Effect
  </div>

  <div id="text2">
    Line Two of Text with a Shadow Effect
  </div>
</body>
</html>
```

Listing 3.5 contains a reference to the CSS style sheet `RoundedCorners1.css` that contains three CSS selectors that are applied to the elements whose id attribute has value `anchor`, `text1`, and `text2`, respectively. The CSS selectors defined in `RoundedCorners1.css` create visual effects, and as you will see, the `hover` pseudoselector enables you to create animation effects.

LISTING 3.6 `RoundedCorners1.css`

```
a.anchor:hover {
background: #00F;
}

a.anchor {
background: #FF0;
font-size: 24px;
font-weight: bold;
padding: 4px 4px;
color: rgba(255,0,0,0.8);
text-shadow: 0 1px 1px rgba(0,0,0,0.4);
-webkit-transition: all 2.0s ease;
-transition: all 2.0s ease;
-webkit-border-radius: 8px;
border-radius: 8px;
}

#text1 {
   font-size: 24pt;
   text-shadow: 2px 4px 5px #00f;
}

#text2 {
   font-size: 32pt;
   text-shadow: 4px 5px 6px #f00;
}

#round1 {
   -moz-border-radius-bottomleft: 20px;
   -moz-border-radius-bottomright: 20px;
   -moz-border-radius-topleft: 20px;
   -moz-border-radius-topright: 20px;
   -moz-box-shadow: 2px 2px 10px #ccc;
   -webkit-border-bottom-left-radius: 20px;
   -webkit-border-bottom-right-radius: 20px;
   -webkit-border-top-left-radius: 20px;
   -webkit-border-top-right-radius: 20px;
   -webkit-box-shadow: 2px 2px 10px #ccc;
   background-color: #f00;
   margin: 25px auto 0;
   padding: 25px 10px;
   text-align: center;
   width: 260px;
}
```

Listing 3.6 contains the selector a.anchor:hover that changes the text color from yellow (#FF0) to blue (#00F) during a two-second interval when users hover over any anchor element with their mouse.

The selector a.anchor contains various attributes that specify the dimensions of the box that encloses the text in the <a> element, along with two new pairs of attributes. The first pair specifies the transition attribute (and a WebKit-specific prefix), which we will discuss later in this chapter. The second pair specifies the border-radius attribute (and the WebKit-specific attribute) whose value is 8px, which determines the radius (in pixels) of the rounded corners of the box that encloses the text in the <a> element. The last two selectors are identical to the selectors in Listing 3.1. Figure 3.3 displays the result of applying the CSS style sheet RoundedCorners1.css to the elements in the HTML page RoundedCorners1.html.

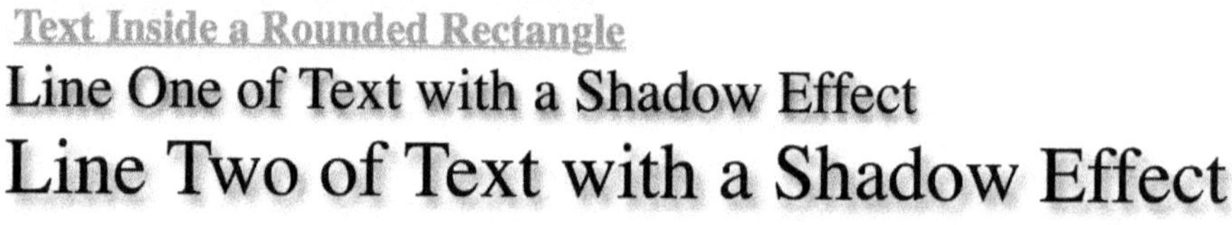

Text Inside a Rounded Rectangle
Line One of Text with a Shadow Effect
Line Two of Text with a Shadow Effect

FIGURE 3.3 CSS3 rounded corners effect.

CSS3 GRADIENTS

CSS3 supports linear gradients and radial gradients, which enable you to create gradient effects that are as visually rich as gradients in other technologies such as SVG and Silverlight. The code samples in this section illustrate how to define linear gradients and radial gradients in CSS3 and then apply them to HTML elements.

Linear Gradients

CSS3 linear gradients require you to specify one or more "color stops," each of which specifies a start color, and end color, and a rendering pattern. WebKit-based browsers support the following syntax to define a linear gradient:

- a start point
- an end point
- a start color using from()
- zero or more stop-colors
- an end color using to()

A start point can be specified as an (x,y) pair of numbers or percentages. For example, the pair (100, 25%) specifies the point that is 100 pixels to the right of the origin and 25% of the way down from the top of the screen. Recall that the origin is located in the upper-left corner of the screen. Listing 3.7 displays the contents of LinearGradient1.html and Listing 3.8 displays the contents of LinearGradient1.css, which illustrate how to apply linear gradients to text strings that are enclosed in <p> elements and an <h3> element.

LISTING 3.7 LinearGradient1.html

```
<!doctype html>
<html lang="en">
<head>
  <title>CSS Linear Gradient Example</title>
  <meta charset="utf-8" />
  <link href="LinearGradient1.css" rel="stylesheet"
                                  type="text/css">
</head>

<body>
  <div id="outer">
    <p id="line1">line 1 with a linear gradient</p>
    <p id="line2">line 2 with a linear gradient</p>
    <p id="line3">line 3 with a linear gradient</p>
    <p id="line4">line 4 with a linear gradient</p>
    <p id="outline">line 5 with Shadow Outline</p>
    <h3><a href="#">A Line of Gradient Text</a></h3>
  </div>
</body>
</html>
```

Listing 3.7 is a simple Web page containing four <p> elements and one <h3> element. Listing 3.7 also references the CSS style sheet LinearGradient1.css that contains CSS selectors that are applied to the four <p> elements and the <h3> element in Listing 3.7.

LISTING 3.8 LinearGradient1.css

```
#line1 {
width: 50%;
font-size: 32px;
background-image: -webkit-gradient(linear, 0% 0%, 0% 100%,
                          from(#fff), to(#f00));
background-image: -gradient(linear, 0% 0%, 0% 100%,
                          from(#fff), to(#f00));
-webkit-border-radius: 4px;
```

```
border-radius: 4px;
}

#line2 {
width: 50%;
font-size: 32px;
background-image: -webkit-gradient(linear, 100% 0%, 0% 100%,
                            from(#fff), to(#ff0));
background-image: -gradient(linear, 100% 0%, 0% 100%,
                       from(#fff), to(#ff0));
-webkit-border-radius: 4px;
border-radius: 4px;
}

#line3 {
width: 50%;
font-size: 32px;
background-image: -webkit-gradient(linear, 0% 0%, 0% 100%,
                            from(#f00), to(#00f));
background-image: -gradient(linear, 0% 0%, 0% 100%,
                       from(#f00), to(#00f));
-webkit-border-radius: 4px;
border-radius: 4px;
}

#line4 {
width: 50%;
font-size: 32px;
background-image: -webkit-gradient(linear, 100% 0%, 0% 100%,
                            from(#f00), to(#00f));
background-image: -gradient(linear, 100% 0%, 0% 100%,
                       from(#f00), to(#00f));
-webkit-border-radius: 4px;
border-radius: 4px;
}

#outline {
font-size: 2.0em;
font-weight: bold;
color: #fff;
text-shadow: 1px 1px 1px rgba(0,0,0,0.5);
}

h3 {
width: 50%;
position: relative;
margin-top: 0;
font-size: 32px;
font-family: helvetica, ariel;
}
```

```
h3 a {
position: relative;
color: red;
text-decoration: none;
-webkit-mask-image: -webkit-gradient(linear, left top,
                        left bottom, from(rgba(0,0,0,1)),
                        color-stop(50%, rgba(0,0,0,0.5)),
                        to(rgba(0,0,0,0))));
}
```

```
h3:after {
content:"This is a Line of Gradient Text";
color: blue;
}
```

The first selector in Listing 3.8 specifies a `font-size` of 32 for text, a `border-radius` of 4 (which renders rounded corners), and a linear gradient that varies from white to blue, as shown here:

```
#line1 {
width: 50%;
font-size: 32px;
background-image: -webkit-gradient(linear, 0% 0%, 0% 100%,
                        from(#fff), to(#f00));
background-image: -gradient(linear, 0% 0%, 0% 100%,
                        from(#fff), to(#f00));
-webkit-border-radius: 4px;
border-radius: 4px;
}
```

As you can see, the first selector contains two attributes with a -webkit- prefix and two standard attributes without this prefix. Because the next three selectors in Listing 3.8 are similar to the first selector, we will not discuss their content.

The next CSS selector creates a text outline with a nice shadow effect by rendering the text in white with a thin black shadow, as shown here:

```
color: #fff;

text-shadow: 1px 1px 1px rgba(0,0,0,0.5);
```

The final portion of Listing 3.8 contains three selectors that affect the rendering of the <h3> element and its embedded <a> element: the h3 selector specifies the width and font size; the h3 a selector specifies a linear gradient; and the h3:after selector specifies the text string to display. Note that other attributes are specified, but these are the main attributes for these selectors. Figure 3.4 displays the result of applying the selectors in the CSS style sheet LinearGradient1.css to the HTML page LinearGradient1.html.

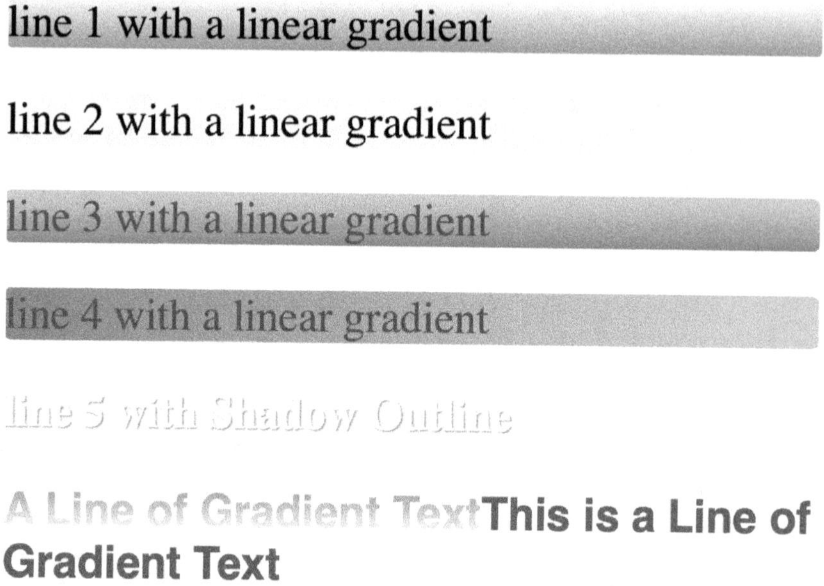

line 1 with a linear gradient

line 2 with a linear gradient

line 3 with a linear gradient

line 4 with a linear gradient

line 5 with Shadow Outline

A Line of Gradient Text**This is a Line of Gradient Text**

FIGURE 3.4 CSS3 linear gradient effect.

Radial Gradients

CSS3 radial gradients are more complex than CSS3 linear gradients, but you can use them to create more complex gradient effects. WebKit-based browsers support the following syntax to define a radial gradient:

- a start point
- a start radius
- an end point
- an end radius
- a start color using `from()`
- zero or more stop-colors
- an end color using `to()`

Notice that the syntax for a radial gradient is similar to the syntax for a linear gradient, except that you also specify a start radius and an end radius. Listing 3.9 displays the contents of `RadialGradient1.html` and Listing 3.10 displays the contents of `RadialGradient1.css`, which illustrate how to render various circles with radial gradients.

LISTING 3.9 `RadialGradient1.html`

```
<!doctype html>
<html lang="en">
<head>
```

```
<title>CSS Radial Gradient Example</title>
<meta charset="utf-8" />
<link href="RadialGradient9.css" rel="stylesheet"
                                   type="text/css">
</head>

<body>
 <div id="outer">
  <div id="radial3">Text3</div>
  <div id="radial2">Text2</div>
  <div id="radial4">Text4</div>
  <div id="radial1">Text1</div>
 </div>
</body>
</html>
```

Listing 3.9 contains five <div> elements whose id attribute has value
outer, radial1, radial2, radial3, and radial4, respectively. Listing 3.9
also references the CSS style sheet RadialGradient1.css that contains five
CSS selectors that are applied to the five <div> elements.

LISTING 3.10 RadialGradient1.css

```
#outer {
position: relative; top: 10px; left: 0px;
}

#radial1 {
font-size: 24px;
width:  300px;
height: 300px;
position: absolute; top: 300px; left: 300px;

background: -webkit-gradient(
  radial, 500 40%, 0, 301 25%, 360, from(red),
  color-stop(0.05, orange), color-stop(0.4, yellow),
  color-stop(0.6, green), color-stop(0.8, blue),
  to(#fff)
 );
}

#radial2 {
font-size: 24px;
width:  500px;
height: 500px;
position: absolute; top: 100px; left: 100px;

background: -webkit-gradient(
  radial, 500 40%, 0, 301 25%, 360, from(red),
  color-stop(0.05, orange), color-stop(0.4, yellow),
  color-stop(0.6, green), color-stop(0.8, blue),
```

```
  to(#fff)
 );
}


#radial3 {
font-size: 24px;
width:   600px;
height: 600px;
position: absolute; top: 0px; left: 0px;

background: -webkit-gradient(
   radial, 500 40%, 0, 301 25%, 360, from(red),
   color-stop(0.05, orange), color-stop(0.4, yellow),
   color-stop(0.6, green), color-stop(0.8, blue),
   to(#fff)
 );
-webkit-box-shadow:  0px 0px 8px #000;
}


#radial4 {
font-size: 24px;
width:   400px;
height: 400px;
position: absolute; top: 200px; left: 200px;

background: -webkit-gradient(
   radial, 500 40%, 0, 301 25%, 360, from(red),
   color-stop(0.05, orange), color-stop(0.4, yellow),
   color-stop(0.6, green), color-stop(0.8, blue),
   to(#fff)
 );
}
```

The first part of the #radial1 selector in Listing 3.10 contains the attributes width and height that specify the dimensions of a rendered rectangle, and also a position attribute that is similar to the position attribute in the #outer selector. The #radial1 also contains a background attribute that defines a radial gradient using the -webkit- prefix, as shown here:

```
background: -webkit-gradient(
   radial, 100 25%, 20, 100 25%, 40, from(blue), to(#fff)
 );
```

The preceding radial gradient specifies the following:
- a start point of (100, 25%)
- a start radius of 20
- an end point of (100, 25%)
- an end radius of 40
- a start color of blue
- an end color of white (#fff)

Notice that the start point and end point are the same, which renders a set of concentric circles that vary from blue to white.

The other four selectors in Listing 3.10 have the same syntax as the first selector, but the rendered radial gradients are significantly different. You can create these and other effects by specifying different start points and end points, and by specifying a start radius that is larger than the end radius.

The `#radial4` selector creates a ringed effect by means of two `stop-color` attributes, as shown here:

```
color-stop(0.2, orange), color-stop(0.4, yellow),

color-stop(0.6, green), color-stop(0.8, blue),
```

You can add additional stop-color attributes to create more complex radial gradients.

Figure 3.5 displays the result of applying the selectors in the CSS style sheet `RadialGradient1.css` to the HTML page `RadialGradient1.html`.

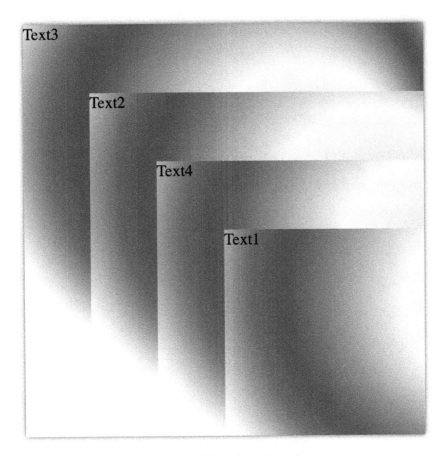

FIGURE 3.5 CSS3 radial gradient effect.

CSS3 2D TRANSFORMS

In addition to transitions, CSS3 supports four transforms that you can apply to 2D shapes and also to PNG files. The four CSS3 transforms are `scale`, `rotate`, `skew`, and `translate`. The following sections contain code samples that illustrate how to apply each of these CSS3 transforms to a set of PNG files. The animation effects occur when users hover over any of the PNG files; moreover, you can create partial animation effects by moving your mouse quickly between adjacent PNG files.

Zoom Effects With Scale Transforms

The CSS3 `transform` attribute allows you to specify the `scale()` function in order to create zoom in/out effects, and the syntax for the `scale()` method looks like this:

```
scale(someValue);
```

You can replace `someValue` with any nonzero number. When `someValue` is between 0 and 1, you will reduce the size of the 2D shape or PNG file, creating a "zoom out" effect; values greater than 1 for `someValue` will increase the size of the 2D shape or PNG file, creating a "zoom in" effect; and a value of 1 does not perform any changes.

Listing 3.11 displays the contents of `Scale1.html` and Listing 3.12 displays the contents of `Scale1.css`, which illustrate how to scale PNG files to create a "hover box" image gallery.

LISTING 3.11 `Scale1.html`

```
<!DOCTYPE html>
<html lang="en">
<head>
  <title>CSS Scale Transform Example</title>
  <meta charset="utf-8" />
  <link href="Scale1.css" rel="stylesheet" type="text/css">
</head>

<body>
  <header>
   <h1>Hover Over any of the Images:</h1>
  </header>

  <div id="outer">
    <img src="Clown1.png"     class="scaled" width="150"
                                              height="150"/>
     <img src="Avocadoes1.png" class="scaled" width="150"
                                              height="150"/>
```

```
<img src="Clown1.png"    class="scaled" width="150"
                                         height="150"/>
<img src="Avocadoes1.png" class="scaled" width="150"
                                         height="150"/>
</div>

</body>
</html>
```

Listing 3.11 references the CSS style sheet Scale1.css, which contains selectors for creating scaled effects, and four HTML <img> elements that reference the PNG files Clown1.png and Avocadoes1.png. The remainder of Listing 3.12 is straightforward, with simple boilerplate text and HTML elements.

LISTING 3.12 Scale1.css

```
#outer {
float: left;
position: relative; top: 50px; left: 50px;
}

img {
-webkit-transition: -webkit-transform 1.0s ease;
-transition: transform 1.0s ease;
}

img.scaled {
  -webkit-box-shadow: 10px 10px 5px #800;
  box-shadow: 10px 10px 5px #800;
}

img.scaled:hover {
-webkit-transform : scale(2);
-transform : scale(2);
}
```

The img selector in Listing 3.12 specifies a transition property that contains a transform effect that occurs during a one-second interval using the ease function, as shown here:

```
-transition: transform 1.0s ease;
```

Next, the selector img.scaled specifies a box-shadow property that creates a reddish shadow effect (seen in Figure 3.6), as shown here:

```
img.scaled {
  -webkit-box-shadow: 10px 10px 5px #800;
  box-shadow: 10px 10px 5px #800;
}
```

Finally, the selector img.scaled:hover specifies a transform attribute that uses the scale() function in order to double the size of the associated PNG file when users hover over any of the <img> elements with their mouse, as shown here:

```
-transform : scale(2);
```

Because the img selector specifies a one-second interval using an ease function, the scaling effect will last for one second. Experiment with different values for the CSS3 scale() function and also different values for the time interval to create the animation effects that suit your needs.

Another point to remember is that you can scale both horizontally and vertically:

```
img {
-webkit-transition: -webkit-transform 1.0s ease;
-transition: transform 1.0s ease;
}

img.mystyle:hover {
-webkit-transform : scaleX(1.5) scaleY(0.5);
-transform : scaleX(1.5) scaleY(0.5);
}
```

Figure 3.6 displays the result of applying the selectors in the CSS style sheet Scale1.css to the HTML page Scale1.html.

Hover Over any of the Images:

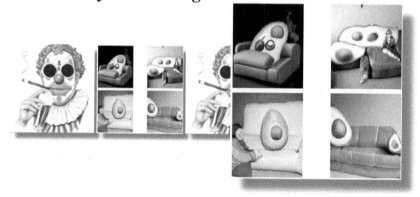

FIGURE 3.6 CSS3 scaling effect.

Rotate Transforms

The CSS3 transform attribute allows you to specify the rotate() function in order to create scaling effects, and its syntax looks like this:

```
rotate(someValue);
```

You can replace `someValue` with any number. When `someValue` is positive, the rotation is clockwise; when `someValue` is negative, the rotation is counterclockwise; and when `someValue` is zero, there is no rotation effect. In all cases the initial position for the rotation effect is the positive horizontal axis. Listing 3.13 displays the contents of `Rotate1.html`, and Listing 3.14 displays the contents of `Rotate1.css`, which illustrate how to rotate PNG files in opposite directions.

LISTING 3.13 `Rotate1.html`

```html
<!DOCTYPE html>
<html lang="en">
<head>
  <title>CSS Rotate Transform Example</title>
  <meta charset="utf-8" />
  <link href="Rotate1.css" rel="stylesheet" type="text/css">
</head>

<body>
  <header>
   <h1>Hover Over any of the Images:</h1>
  </header>

  <div id="outer">
    <img src="Clown1.png"     class="imageL" width="150"
                                              height="150"/>
    <img src="Avocadoes1.png" class="imageR" width="150"
                                              height="150"/>
    <img src="Clown1.png"     class="imageL" width="150"
                                              height="150"/>
    <img src="Avocadoes1.png" class="imageR" width="150"
                                              height="150"/>
  </div>
</body>
</html>
```

Listing 3.13 references the CSS style sheet `Rotate1.css`, which contains selectors for creating rotation effects, and an HTML `<img>` element that references the PNG files `Clown1.png` and `Avocadoes1.png`. The remainder of Listing 3.13 consists of simple boilerplate text and HTML elements.

LISTING 3.14 `Rotate1.css`

```css
#outer {
float: left;
position: relative; top: 100px; left: 150px;
}
```

```
img {
-webkit-transition: -webkit-transform 1.0s ease;
-transition: transform 1.0s ease;
}

img.imageL {
  -webkit-box-shadow: 14px 14px 8px #800;
  box-shadow: 14px 14px 8px #800;
}

img.imageR {
  -webkit-box-shadow: 14px 14px 8px #008;
  box-shadow: 14px 14px 8px #008;
}

img.imageL:hover {
-webkit-transform : scale(2) rotate(-45deg);
-transform : scale(2) rotate(-45deg);
}

img.imageR:hover {
-webkit-transform : scale(2) rotate(360deg);
-transform : scale(2) rotate(360deg);
}
```

Listing 3.14 contains the img selector that specifies a transition attribute that creates an animation effect during a one-second interval using the ease timing function, as shown here:

```
-transition: transform 1.0s ease;
```

Next, the selectors img.imageL and img.imageR contain a property that renders a reddish and bluish background shadow, respectively.

The selector img.imageL:hover specifies a transform attribute that performs a counterclockwise scaling effect (doubling the original size) and a rotation effect (45-degrees counterclockwise) when users hover over the <img> element with their mouse, as shown here:

```
-transform : scale(2) rotate(-45deg);
```

The selector img.imageR:hover is similar, except that it performs a clockwise rotation of 360 degrees. Figure 3.7 displays the result of applying the selectors in the CSS style sheet Rotate1.css to the elements in the HTML page Rotate1.html.

Hover Over any of the Images:

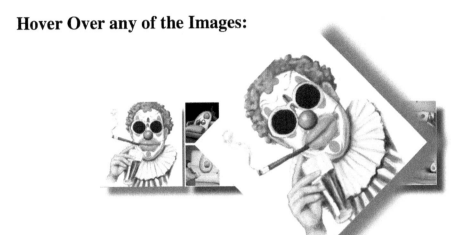

FIGURE 3.7 CSS3 rotation effect.

Skew Transforms

The CSS3 transform attribute allows you to specify the skew() function in order to create skewing effects, and its syntax looks like this:

```
skew(xAngle, yAngle);
```

You can replace xAngle and yAngle with any number. When xAngle and yAngle are positive, the skew effect is clockwise; when xAngle and yAngle are negative, the skew effect is counterclockwise; and when xAngle and yAngle are zero, there is no skew effect. In all cases the initial position for the skew effect is the positive horizontal axis. Listing 3.15 displays the contents of Skew1.html and Listing 3.16 displays the contents of Skew1.css, which illustrate how to skew a PNG file.

LISTING 3.15 Skew1.html

```
<!DOCTYPE html>
<html lang="en">
<head>
  <title>CSS Skew Transform Example</title>
  <meta charset="utf-8" />
  <link href="Skew1.css" rel="stylesheet" type="text/css">
</head>

<body>
```

```
<header>
 <h1>Hover Over any of the Images:</h1>
</header>

<div id="outer">
 <img src="Clown1.png"       class="skewed1" width="150"
                                             height="150"/>
  <img src="Avocadoes1.png" class="skewed2" width="150"
                                             height="150"/>
  <img src="Clown1.png"       class="skewed3" width="150"
                                             height="150"/>
  <img src="Avocadoes1.png" class="skewed4" width="150"
                                             height="150"/>
</div>

</body>
</html>
```

Listing 3.15 references the CSS style sheet Skew1.css, which contains selectors for creating skew effects, and an <img> element that references the PNG files Clown1.png and Avocadoes1.png. The remainder of Listing 3.15 consists of simple boilerplate text and HTML elements.

LISTING 3.16 Skew1.html

```
#outer {
float: left;
position: relative; top: 100px; left: 100px;
}

img {
-webkit-transition: -webkit-transform 1.0s ease;
-transition: transform 1.0s ease;
}

img.skewed1 {
  -webkit-box-shadow: 14px 14px 8px #800;
  box-shadow: 14px 14px 8px #800;
}

img.skewed2 {
  -webkit-box-shadow: 14px 14px 8px #880;
  box-shadow: 14px 14px 8px #880;
}

img.skewed3 {
  -webkit-box-shadow: 14px 14px 8px #080;
  box-shadow: 14px 14px 8px #080;
}

img.skewed4 {
```

```
    -webkit-box-shadow: 14px 14px 8px #008;
    box-shadow: 14px 14px 8px #008;
}


img.skewed1:hover {
-webkit-transform : scale(2) skew(-10deg, -30deg);
-transform : scale(2) skew(-10deg, -30deg);
}


img.skewed2:hover {
-webkit-transform : scale(2) skew(10deg, 30deg);
-transform : scale(2) skew(10deg, 30deg);
}


img.skewed3:hover {
-webkit-transform : scale(0.4) skew(-10deg, -30deg);
-transform : scale(0.4) skew(-10deg, -30deg);
}


img.skewed4:hover {
-webkit-transform : scale(0.5, 1.5) skew(10deg, -30deg);
-transform : scale(0.5, 1.5) skew(10deg, -30deg);
opacity:0.5;
}
```

Listing 3.16 contains the img selector that specifies a transition attribute that creates an animation effect during a one-second interval using the ease timing function, as shown here:

```
-transition: transform 1.0s ease;
```

The four selectors img.skewed1, img.skewed2, img.skewed3, and img. skewed4 create background shadow effects with darker shades of red, yellow, green, and blue, respectively (all of which you have seen in earlier code samples). The selector img.skewed1:hover specifies a transform attribute that performs a skew effect when users hover over the first <img> element with their mouse, as shown here:

```
-transform : scale(2) skew(-10deg, -30deg);
```

The other three CSS3 selectors also use a combination of the CSS functions skew() and scale() to create distinct visual effects. Notice that the fourth hover selector also sets the opacity property to 0.5, which is applied in parallel with the other effects in this selector. Figure 3.8 displays the result of applying the selectors in the CSS style sheet Skew1.css to the elements in the HTML page Skew1.html.

Hover Ove̶ ̶ ̶y of the Images:

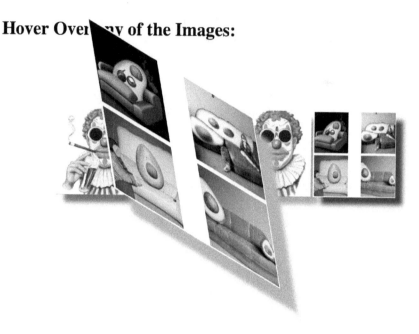

FIGURE 3.8 CSS3 skew effect.

Translate Transforms

The CSS3 transform attribute allows you to specify the `translate()` function in order to create translation or "shifting" effects, and its syntax looks like this:

```
translate(xDirection, yDirection);
```

The translation is in relation to the origin, which is the upper-left corner of the screen. Thus, positive values for `xDirection` and `yDirection` produce a shift toward the right and a shift downward, respectively, whereas negative values for `xDirection` and `yDirection` produce a shift toward the left and a shift upward; zero values for `xDirection` and `yDirection` do not cause any translation effect. Listing 3.17 displays the contents of `Translate1.html` and Listing 3.18 displays the contents of `Translate1.css`, which illustrate how to apply a translation effect to a PNG file.

LISTING 3.17 `Translate1.html`

```
<!DOCTYPE html>
<html lang="en">
<head>
  <title>CSS Translate Transform Example</title>
  <meta charset="utf-8" />
  <link href="Translate1.css" rel="stylesheet"
                              type="text/css">
</head>
```

```
<body>
  <header>
  <h1>Hover Over any of the Images:</h1>
  </header>

  <div id="outer">
    <img src="Clown1.png"      class="trans1" width="150"
                                               height="150"/>
      <img src="Avocadoes1.png" class="trans2" width="150"
                                               height="150"/>
      <img src="Clown1.png"      class="trans3" width="150"
                                               height="150"/>
      <img src="Avocadoes1.png" class="trans4" width="150"
                                               height="150"/>
  </div>
</body>
</html>
```

Listing 3.17 references the CSS style sheet `Translate1.css`, which contains selectors for creating translation effects, and an `<img>` element that references the PNG files `Clown1.png` and `Avocadoes1.png`. The remainder of Listing 3.17 consists of straightforward boilerplate text and HTML elements.

LISTING 3.18 `Translate1.css`

```
#outer {
float: left;
position: relative; top: 100px; left: 100px;
}

img {
-webkit-transition: -webkit-transform 1.0s ease;
-transition: transform 1.0s ease;
}

img.trans1 {
  -webkit-box-shadow: 14px 14px 8px #800;
  box-shadow: 14px 14px 8px #800;
}

img.trans2 {
  -webkit-box-shadow: 14px 14px 8px #880;
  box-shadow: 14px 14px 8px #880;
}

img.trans3 {
  -webkit-box-shadow: 14px 14px 8px #080;
  box-shadow: 14px 14px 8px #080;
}
```

```
img.trans4 {
  -webkit-box-shadow: 14px 14px 8px #008;
  box-shadow: 14px 14px 8px #008;
}

img.trans1:hover {
-webkit-transform : scale(2) translate(100px, 50px);
-transform : scale(2) translate(100px, 50px);
}

img.trans2:hover {
-webkit-transform : scale(0.5) translate(-50px, -50px);
-transform : scale(0.5) translate(-50px, -50px);
}

img.trans3:hover {
-webkit-transform : scale(0.5,1.5) translate(0px, 0px);
-transform : scale(0.5,1.5) translate(0px, 0px);
}

img.trans4:hover {
-webkit-transform : scale(2) translate(50px, -50px);
-transform : scale(2) translate(100px, 50px);
}
```

Listing 3.17 contains the img selector that specifies a transform effect during a one-second interval using the ease timing function, as shown here:

```
-transition: transform 1.0s ease;
```

The four selectors img.trans1, img.trans2, img.trans3, and img. trans4 create background shadow effects with darker shades of red, yellow, green, and blue, respectively, just as you saw in the previous section.

The selector img.trans1:hover specifies a transform attribute that performs a scale effect and a translation effect when users hover over the first <img> element with their mouse, as shown here:

```
-webkit-transform : scale(2) translate(100px, 50px);
transform : scale(2) translate(100px, 50px);
```

The other three selectors contain similar code involving a combination of a translate and a scaling effect, each of which creates a distinct visual effect. Figure 3.9 displays the result of applying the selectors defined in the CSS3 style sheet Translate1.css to the elements in the HTML page Translate1.html.

Hover Over any of the Images:

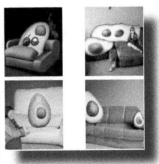

FIGURE 3.9 PNG files with CSS3 scale and translate effects.

SUMMARY

This chapter showed you how to create graphics effects, shadow effects, and how to use CSS3 transforms in CSS3. You learned how to create animation effects that you can apply to HTML elements. You saw how to define CSS3 selectors to do the following:

* render rounded rectangles
* create shadow effects for text and 2D shapes
* create linear and radial gradients
* use the methods `translate()`, `rotate()`, `skew()`, and `scale()`
* create CSS3-based animation effects

NOTE

[1] In regard to the terminology in this book, although every attempt to be consistent was made, there are times when terminology is not 100% correct. For example, WebKit is an engine and not a browser. Therefore, "WebKit-based browser" is correct, whereas "WebKit browser" is incorrect, but you will see both used (even though only the former is technically correct). Second, you will see "HTML Web page" and "HTML page" used interchangeably. Third, sometimes references to HTML elements do not specify "HTML," so you will see "<p> element" and "HTML <p> element" (or some other HTML element) in the discussion that precedes or follows a code sample. Please keep the preceding points in mind so there won't be any confusion as you read through the volume.

CSS3 3D ANIMATION

T his chapter continues the discussion of CSS3 that began in Chapter 2, with a focus on examples of creating 3D effects and 3D animation effects.

The first section of this chapter shows you how to display a CSS3-based cube, followed by examples of CSS3 transitions for creating simple animation effects, such as glow effects and bouncing effects. Specifically, you will learn how to use CSS3 `keyframe` and the CSS3 functions `scale3d()`, `rotate3d()`, and `translate3d()` that enable you to create 3D animation effects.

The second section of this chapter contains examples of creating glowing effects, fading image effects, and bouncing effects. You will also see how to create CSS3 effects for text and how to render multicolumn text.

The third section of this chapter briefly discusses CSS3 media queries, which enable you to render a given HTML page based on the properties of the device.

Keep in mind that you can also use JavaScript in order to create visual effects that can be easier than using CSS3 alone. Moreover, you can use CSS3 media queries for rendering HMTL pages differently on different mobile devices. Neither of these topics is covered in this book, but an Internet search will provide various links and tutorials that contain information on these topics.

A CSS3-BASED CUBE

You can use the CSS3 transforms `rotate()`, `scale()`, and `skew()` in order to create and render a 3D cube with gradient shading. Listing 4.1 displays the contents of `3DCubeHover1.html` and Listing 4.2 displays the contents of `3DCubeHover1.css`, which illustrate how to simulate a cube in CSS3.

LISTING 4.1 `3DCubeHover1.html`

```
<!DOCTYPE html>
<html lang="en">
<head>
<title>CSS 3D Cube Example</title>
 <meta charset="utf-8" />
   <link href="3DCSS1.css" rel="stylesheet" type="text/css">
</head>

<body>
  <header>
   <h1>Hover Over the Cube Faces:</h1>
  </header>

 <div id="outer">
  <div id="top">Text1</div>
  <div id="left">Text2</div>
  <div id="right">Text3</div>
 </div>
</body>
</html>
```

Listing 4.1 is a straightforward HTML page that references the CSS style
sheet `3DCSS1.css` that contains the CSS3 selectors for styling the HTML
`<div>` elements in this Web page.

LISTING 4.2 `3DCSS1.css`

```
/* animation effects */
#right:hover {
-webkit-transition: -webkit-transform 3.0s ease;
-transition: transform 3.0s ease;

-webkit-transform : scale(1.2) skew(-10deg, -30deg)
                                        rotate(-45deg);
-transform : scale(1.2) skew(-10deg, -30deg) rotate(-45deg);
}

#left:hover {
-webkit-transition: -webkit-transform 2.0s ease;
-transition: transform 2.0s ease;

-webkit-transform : scale(0.8) skew(-10deg, -30deg)
                                        rotate(-45deg);
-transform : scale(0.8) skew(-10deg, -30deg) rotate(-45deg);
}

#top:hover {
-webkit-transition: -webkit-transform 2.0s ease;
-transition: transform 2.0s ease;
```

```
-webkit-transform : scale(0.5) skew(-20deg, -30deg)
                                       rotate(45deg);
-transform : scale(0.5) skew(-20deg, -30deg) rotate(45deg);
}

/* size and position */
#right, #left, #top {
position:relative;  padding: 0px;  width: 200px;
                                       height: 200px;

}

#left {
  font-size: 48px;
  left: 20px;

  background-image:
    -webkit-radial-gradient(red 4px, transparent 28px),
    -webkit-repeating-radial-gradient(red 0px,  yellow 4px,
                              green 8px,
                              red 12px, transparent 26px,
                              blue 20px, red 24px,
                              transparent 28px, blue 12px),
    -webkit-repeating-radial-gradient(red 0px,  yellow 4px,
                              green 8px,
                              red 12px, transparent 26px,
                              blue 20px, red 24px,
                              transparent 28px, blue 12px);

  background-size: 100px 40px, 40px 100px;
  background-position: 0 0;

  -webkit-transform: skew(0deg, 30deg);
}

#right {
  font-size: 48px;
  width:  170px;
  top: -192px;
  left: 220px;

  background-image:
    -webkit-radial-gradient(red 4px, transparent 48px),
    -webkit-repeating-linear-gradient(0deg, red 5px,
                              green 4px,
                              yellow 8px, blue 12px,
                              transparent 16px, red 20px,
                              blue 24px, transparent 28px,
                              transparent 32px),
    -webkit-radial-gradient(blue 8px, transparent 68px);

  background-size: 120px 120px, 24px 24px;
  background-position: 0 0;
```

```
        -webkit-transform: skew(0deg, -30deg);
}

#top {
  font-size: 48px;
  top: 50px;
  left: 105px;

  background-image:
    -webkit-radial-gradient(white 2px, transparent 8px),
    -webkit-repeating-linear-gradient(45deg, white 2px,
                        yellow 8px,
                        green 4px, red 12px,
                        transparent 26px, blue 20px,
                        red 24px, transparent 28px,
                        blue 12px),
    -webkit-repeating-linear-gradient(-45deg, white 2px,
                        yellow 8px,
                        green 4px, red 12px,
                        transparent 26px, blue 20px,
                        red 24px, transparent 28px,
                        blue 12px);

  background-size: 100px 30px, 30px 100px;
  background-position: 0 0;

  -webkit-transform: rotate(60deg) skew(0deg, -30deg);
                                    scale(1, 1.16);
}
```

The first three selectors in Listing 4.2 define the animation effects when users hover on the top, left, or right faces of the cube. In particular, the #right:hover selector performs an animation effect during a three-second interval when users hover over the right face of the cube, as shown here:

```
#right:hover {
-webkit-transition: -webkit-transform 3.0s ease;
-transition: transform 3.0s ease;

-webkit-transform : scale(1.2) skew(-10deg, -30deg)
                                    rotate(-45deg);
-transform : scale(1.2) skew(-10deg, -30deg) rotate(-45deg);
}
```

The transition attribute is already familiar to you, and notice that the transform attribute specifies the CSS3 transform functions scale(), skew(), and rotate(), all of which you have seen already in this chapter. These three functions are applied simultaneously, which means that you will see a scaling, skewing, and rotating effect happening at the same time instead of sequentially.

The last three selectors in Listing 4.2 define the properties of each face of the cube. For example, the #left selector specifies the font size for some text and also positional attributes for the left face of the cube. The most complex portion of the #left selector is the value of the background-image attribute, which consists of a WebKit-specific combination of a radial gradient, a repeating radial gradient, and another radial gradient. Notice that the left face is a rectangle that is transformed into a parallelogram using this line of code:

```
-webkit-transform: skew(0deg, -30deg);
```

The #top selector and #right= selector contain code that is comparable to the #left selector, and you can experiment with their values in order to create other visual effects. Figure 4.1 displays the result of applying the CSS selectors in 3DCube1.css to the <div> elements in the HTML page 3DCube1.html.

Hover Over the Cube Faces:

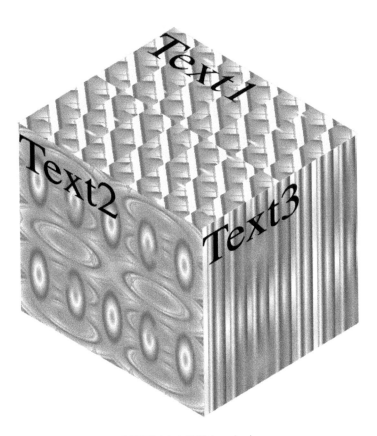

FIGURE 4.1 A CSS3-based cube.

CSS3 TRANSITIONS

CSS3 transitions involve changes to CSS values in a smooth fashion, and they are initiated by user gestures, such as mouse clicks, focus, or hover effects. WebKit originally developed CSS3 transitions, and they are also supported in many versions of Safari, Chrome, Opera, and Firefox by using browser-specific prefixes. Keep in mind that there are toolkits (such as jQuery and Prototype) that support transitions effects similar to their CSS3-based counterparts.

The basic syntax for creating a CSS transition is a "triple" that specifies:

- a CSS property
- a duration (in seconds)
- a transition timing function

Here is an example of a WebKit-based transition:

```
-webkit-transition-property: background;
-webkit-transition-duration: 0.5s;
-webkit-transition-timing-function: ease;
```

Fortunately, you can also combine these transitions in one line, as shown here:

```
-webkit-transition: background 0.5s ease;
```

Here is an example of a CSS3 selector that includes these transitions:

```
a.foo {
padding: 3px 6px;
background: #f00;
-webkit-transition: background 0.5s ease;
}

a.foo:focus, a.foo:hover {
background: #00f;
}
```

Transitions currently require browser-specific prefixes in order for them to work correctly in browsers that are not based on WebKit. Here is an example for Internet Explorer (IE), Firefox, and Opera:

```
-ie-webkit-transition: background 0.5s ease;
-moz-webkit-transition: background 0.5s ease;
-o-webkit-transition: background 0.5s ease;
```

Currently, you can specify one of the following transition timing functions (using browser-specific prefixes):

- ease
- ease-in
- ease-out

- ease-in-out
- cubic-bezier

If these transition functions do not meet your needs, you can create custom functions using this online tool: *www.matthewlein.com/ceaser*. You can specify many properties with –webkit-transition-property, and an extensive list of properties is here:

https://developer.mozilla.org/en/CSS/CSS_transitions.

SIMPLE CSS3 ANIMATION EFFECTS

The CSS3-based code samples that you have seen so far involved primarily static visual effects (although you did see how to use the hover pseudo-selector to create an animation effect). The CSS3 code samples in this section illustrate how to create "glowing" effects and "bouncing" effects for form-based elements.

Glowing Effects

You can combine keyframes and the hover pseudo selector in order to create an animation effect when users hover with their mouse on a specific element in an HTML page. Listing 4.3 displays the contents of Transition1.html and Listing 4.4 displays the contents of Transition1.css, which contains CSS3 selectors that create a glowing effect on an input field.

LISTING 4.3 `Transition1.html`

```
<!DOCTYPE html>
<html lang="en">
<head>
  <title>CSS Animation Example</title>
  <meta charset="utf-8" />
  <link href="Transition1.css" rel="stylesheet"
                               type="text/css">
</head>

<body>
  <div id="outer">
    <input id="input" type="text" value="This is an input
                                   line"></input>
  </div>
</body>
</html>
```

Listing 4.3 is a simple HTML page that contains a reference to the CSS style sheet Transition1.css and one HTML <div> element that contains an <input> field element. As you will see, an animation effect is created when users hover over the <input> element with their mouse.

LISTING 4.4 `Transition1.css`

```
#outer {
position: relative; top: 20px; left: 20px;
}

@-webkit-keyframes glow {
  0% {
    -webkit-box-shadow: 0 0 24px rgba(255, 255, 255, 0.5);
  }
  50% {
    -webkit-box-shadow: 0 0 24px rgba(255, 0, 0, 0.9);
  }
  100% {
    -webkit-box-shadow: 0 0 24px rgba(255, 255, 255, 0.5);
  }
}

#input {
font-size: 24px;
-webkit-border-radius: 4px;
border-radius: 4px;
}

#input:hover {
  -webkit-animation: glow 2.0s 3 ease;
}
```

Listing 4.4 contains a keyframes selector (called "glow") that specifies three shadow effects. The first shadow effect (which occurs at time 0 of the animation effect) renders a white color with an opacity of 0.5. The second shadow effect (at the midway point of the animation effect) renders a red color with an opacity of 0.9. The third shadow effect (which occurs at the end of the animation effect) is identical to the first animation effect.

The #input selector is applied to the input field in `Transition1.html` in order to render a rounded rectangle. The #input:hover selector uses the glow keyframes in order to create an animation effect for a two-second interval, repeated three times, using an ease function, as shown here:

```
-webkit-animation: glow 2.0s 3 ease;
```

Figure 4.2 displays the result of applying the selectors in `Transition1.css` to the elements in the HTML page `Transition1.html`.

FIGURE 4.2 CSS3 glowing transition effect.

Image Fading and Rotating Effects With CSS3

This section shows you how to create a fading effect with JPG images. Listing 4.5 displays the contents of `FadeRotateImages1.html` and Listing 4.6 displays the contents of `FadeRotateImages1.css`, which illustrate how to create a "fading" effect on a JPG file and a glowing effect on another JPG file.

LISTING 4.5 `FadeRotateImages1.html`

```html
<!DOCTYPE html>
<html lang="en">
<head>
  <title>CSS3 Fade and Rotate Images</title>
  <meta charset="utf-8" />
  <link href="FadeRotateImages1.css" rel="stylesheet"
                                    type="text/css">
</head>

<body>
  <div id="outer">
    <img class="lower" width="200" height="200"
                                  src="Clown1.png" />
    <img class="upper" width="200" height="200"
                                  src="Avocadoes1.png" />
  </div>

  <div id="third">
    <img width="200" height="200" src="Clown1.png" />
  </div>
</body>
```

Listing 4.5 contains a reference to the CSS style sheet `FadeRotateImages1.css` that contains CSS selectors for creating a fading effect and a glowing effect. The first HTML `<div>` element in Listing 4.5 contains two `<img>` elements; when users hover over the rendered JPG file, it will "fade" and reveal another JPG file. The second HTML `<div>` element contains one `<img>` element, and when users hover over this JPG, a CSS3 selector will rotate the referenced JPG file around the vertical axis.

LISTING 4.6 `FadeRotateImages1.css`

```css
#outer {
 position: absolute; top: 20px; left: 20px;
 margin: 0 auto;
}

#outer img {
 position:absolute; left:0;
 -webkit-transition: opacity 1s ease-in-out;
```

```
    transition: opacity 1s ease-in-out;
  }

#outer img.upper:hover {
   opacity:0;
}

#third img {
position: absolute; top: 20px; left: 250px;
}

#third img:hover {
 -webkit-animation: rotatey 2.0s 3 ease;
}

@-webkit-keyframes rotatey {
   0% {
     -webkit-transform: rotateY(45deg);
   }
   50% {
     -webkit-transform: rotateY(90deg);
   }
   100% {
     -webkit-transform: rotateY(0);
   }
}
```

We will skip the details of the code in Listing 4.6 that is already familiar to you. The key point for creating the fading effect is to set the opacity value to 0 when users hover over the leftmost image, and the one line of code in the CSS selector is shown here:

```
#outer img.upper:hover {
   opacity:0;
}
```

As you can see, this code sample shows you that it's possible to create attractive visual effects without complicated code or logic.

Next, Listing 4.6 defines a CSS3 selector that creates a rotation effect around the vertical axis by invoking the CSS3 function rotateY() in the keyframe rotatey. Note that you can create a rotation effect about the other two axes by replacing rotateY() with the CSS3 function rotateX() or the CSS3 function rotateZ(). You can even use these three functions in the same keyframe to create 3D effects. CSS3 3D effects are discussed in more detail later in this chapter. Figure 4.3 displays the result of applying the selectors in the CSS style sheet FadeRotateImages1.css to FadeRotateImages1.html.

FIGURE 4.3 CSS3 fade and rotate JPG effects.

Bouncing Effects

This section shows you how to create a "bouncing" animation effect. Listing 4.7 displays the contents of `Bounce2.html` and Listing 4.8 displays the contents of `Bounce2.css`, which illustrate how to create a bouncing effect on an input field.

LISTING 4.7 `Bounce2.html`

```
<!DOCTYPE html>
<html lang="en">
<head>
  <title>CSS Animation Example</title>
  <meta charset="utf-8" />
  <link href="Bounce2.css" rel="stylesheet"
                           type="text/css">
</head>

<body>
  <div id="outer">
    <input id="input" type="text" value="An input line"/ >
  </div>
</body>
</html>
```

Listing 4.7 is another straightforward HTML page that contains a reference to the CSS style sheet `Bounce2.css` and one HTML `<div>` element that contains an `<input>` field element. The CSS style sheet creates a bouncing animation effect when users hover over the `<input>` element with their mouse.

LISTING 4.8 `Bounce2.css`

```css
#outer {
position: relative; top: 50px; left: 100px;
}

@-webkit-keyframes bounce {
  0% {
    left: 50px;
    top: 100px;
    background-color: #ff0000;
  }
  25% {
    left: 100px;
    top: 150px;
    background-color: #ffff00;
  }
  50% {
    left: 50px;
    top: 200px;
    background-color: #00ff00;
  }
  75% {
    left: 0px;
    top: 150px;
    background-color: #0000ff;
  }
  100% {
    left: 50px;
    top: 100px;
    background-color: #ff0000;
  }
}

#input {
font-size: 24px;
-webkit-border-radius: 4px;
border-radius: 4px;
}

#outer:hover {
  -webkit-animation: bounce 2.0s 4 ease;
}
```

Listing 4.8 contains a keyframes selector (called "bounce") that specifies five time intervals: the 0%, 25%, 50%, 75%, and 100% points of the duration of the animation effect. Each time interval specifies values for the attributes left, top, and background color of the `<input>` field. Despite the simplicity of this keyframes selector, it creates a pleasing animation effect.

The `#input` selector is applied to the input field in `Bounce2.html` in order to render a rounded rectangle. The `#input:hover` selector uses the bounce keyframes in order to create an animation effect for a two-second interval, repeated four times, using an ease function, as shown here:

```
-webkit-animation: bounce 2.0s 4 ease;
```

Figure 4.4 displays the result of applying the selectors in the CSS style sheet `Bounce2.css` to the elements in the HTML page `Bounce2.html`.

An input line

FIGURE 4.4 CSS3 bouncing animation effect.

CSS3 EFFECTS FOR TEXT

You have seen examples of rendering text strings as part of several code samples in the previous chapter, and in this section we discuss a new feature of CSS3 that enables you to render text in multiple columns.

Rendering Multicolumn Text

CSS3 supports multicolumn text, which can create a nice visual effect when a Web page contains significant amounts of text. Listing 4.9 displays the contents of `MultiColumns1.html` and Listing 4.10 displays the contents of `MultiColumns1.css` that illustrate how to render multicolumn text.

LISTING 4.9 `MultiColumns1.html`

```
<!doctype html>
<html lang="en">
<head>
  <title>CSS Multi Columns Example</title>
  <meta charset="utf-8" />
  <link href="MultiColumns1.css" rel="stylesheet"
                                 type="text/css">
</head>

<body>
  <header>
   <h1>Hover Over the Multi-Column Text:</h1>
  </header>

  <div id="outer">
   <p id="line1">.</p>
```

```
    <article>
     <div id="columns">
       <p> CSS enables you to define selectors that specify
the style or the manner in which you want to render
elements in an HTML page. CSS helps you modularize your
HTML content and since you can place your CSS definitions in
a separate file, you can also reuse the same CSS definitions
in multiple HTML files.
       </p>
       <p> Moreover, CSS also enables you to simplify the
updates that you need to make to elements in HTML pages.
For example, suppose that multiple HTML table elements use
a CSS rule that specifies the color red. If you later need
to change the color to blue, you can effect such a change
simply by making one change (i.e., changing red to blue) in
one CSS rule.
       </p>
       <p> Without a CSS rule, you would be forced to
manually update the color attribute in every HTML table
element that is affected, which is error-prone, time-
consuming, and extremely inefficient.
       <p>
     </div>
    </article>
    <p id="line1">.</p>
   </div>
</body>
</html>
```

The HTML Web page in Listing 4.9 contains semantic tags for rendering the text in several HTML <p> elements. As you can see, this HTML5 page is straightforward, and the multicolumn effects are defined in the CSS style sheet MultiColumns1.css that is displayed in Listing 4.10.

LISTING 4.10 MultiColumns1.css

```
/* animation effects */
#columns:hover {
-webkit-transition: -webkit-transform 3.0s ease;
-transition: transform 3.0s ease;

-webkit-transform : scale(0.5) skew(-20deg, -30deg)
rotate(45deg);
-transform : scale(0.5) skew(-20deg, -30deg) rotate(45deg);
}

#line1:hover {
-webkit-transition: -webkit-transform 3.0s ease;
-transition: transform 3.0s ease;
```

```
-webkit-transform : scale(0.5) skew(-20deg, -30deg)
                                        rotate(45deg);
-transform : scale(0.5) skew(-20deg, -30deg) rotate(45deg);
background-image: -webkit-gradient(linear, 0% 0%, 0% 100%,
                                from(#fff), to(#00f));
background-image: -gradient(linear, 0% 0%, 0% 100%,
                                from(#fff), to(#00f));
-webkit-border-radius: 8px;border-radius: 8px;}


#columns {
-webkit-column-count : 3;
-webkit-column-gap : 80px;
-webkit-column-rule : 1px solid rgb(255,255,255);
column-count : 3;
column-gap : 80px;
column-rule : 1px solid rgb(255,255,255);
}


#line1 {
color: red;
font-size: 24px;
background-image: -webkit-gradient(linear, 0% 0%, 0% 100%,
                                from(#fff), to(#f00));
background-image: -gradient(linear, 0% 0%, 0% 100%,
                                from(#fff), to(#f00));
-webkit-border-radius: 4px;border-radius: 4px;
}
```

The first two selectors in Listing 4.10 create an animation effect when users hover over the `<div>` elements whose id attribute is `columns` or `line1`. Both selectors create an animation effect during a three-second interval using the CSS3 functions `scale()`, `skew()`, and `rotate()`, as shown here:

```
-webkit-transition: -webkit-transform 3.0s ease;
-transition: transform 3.0s ease;
-webkit-transform : scale(0.5) skew(-20deg, -30deg)
                                        rotate(45deg);
```

The second selector also defines a linear gradient background effect.

The `#columns` selector in Listing 4.10 contains three layout-related attributes. The `column-count` attribute is 3, so the text is displayed in three columns; the `column-gap` attribute is `80px`, so there is a space of eighty pixels between adjacent columns; the `column-rule` attribute specifies a white background.

The `#line1` selector specifies a linear gradient that creates a nice visual effect above and below the multicolumn text. Figure 4.5 displays the result of applying the CSS selectors in `MultiColumns1.css` to the text in the HTML page `MultiColumns1.html`.

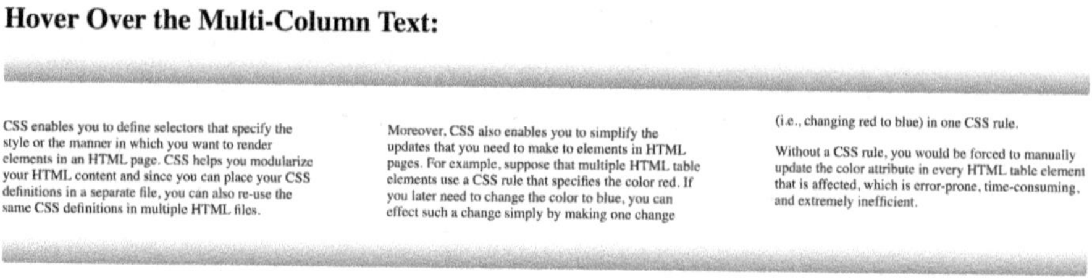

Hover Over the Multi-Column Text:

CSS enables you to define selectors that specify the style or the manner in which you want to render elements in an HTML page. CSS helps you to modularize your HTML content and since you can place your CSS definitions in a separate file, you can also re-use the same CSS definitions in multiple HTML files.

Moreover, CSS also enables you to simplify the updates that you need to make to elements in HTML pages. For example, suppose that multiple HTML table elements use a CSS rule that specifies the color red. If you later need to change the color to blue, you can effect such a change simply by making one change

(i.e., changing red to blue) in one CSS rule. Without a CSS rule, you would be forced to manually update the color attribute in every HTML table element that is affected, which is error-prone, time-consuming, and extremely inefficient.

FIGURE 4.5 Rendering multicolumn text in CSS3.

CSS3 MEDIA QUERIES

CSS3 media queries determine the following attributes of a device:

- browser window width and height
- device width and height
- orientation (landscape or portrait)
- resolution

CSS3 media queries enable you to write mobile applications that will render differently on devices with differing width, height, orientation, and resolution. As a simple example, consider this media query that loads the CSS style sheet `mystuff.css` only if the device is a screen and the maximum width of the device is `480px`:

```
<link rel="stylesheet" type="text/css"
      media="screen and (max-device-width: 480px)"
                                  href="mystuff.css"/>
```

As you can see, this media query contains a media attribute that specifies two components:

- a media type (screen)
- a query (max-device-width: 480px)

The preceding example is a very simple CSS3 media query; fortunately, you can combine multiple components in order to test the values of multiple attributes, as shown in the following pair of CSS3 selectors:

```
@media screen and (max-device-width: 480px) and
                                 (resolution: 160dpi) {
    #innerDiv {
        float: none;
    }
}
@media screen and (min-device-width: 481px) and
                                 (resolution: 160dpi) {
    #innerDiv {
        float: left;
    }
}
```

In the first CSS3 selector, the HTML element whose id attribute has the value innerDiv will have a float property whose value is none on any device whose maximum screen width is 480px. In the second CSS3 selector, the HTML element whose id attribute has the value innerDiv will have a float property whose value is left on any device whose minimum screen width is 481px.

CSS3 3D ANIMATION EFFECTS

As you know by now, CSS3 supports keyframes for creating animation effects (and the duration of those effects) at various points in time. The example in this section uses a CSS3 keyframe and various combinations of the CSS3 functions scale3d(), rotate3d(), and translate3d() in order to create an animation effect that lasts for four minutes. Listing 4.13 displays the contents of the HTML Web page Anim240Flicker3DLGrad4.html, which is a very simple HTML page that contains four <div> elements.

LISTING 4.13 Anim240Flicker3DLGrad4.html

```
<!DOCTYPE html>
<html lang="en">
<head>
  <title>CSS3 Animation Example</title>
  <meta charset="utf-8" />
  <link href="Anim240Flicker3DLGrad4.css"
                  rel="stylesheet" type="text/css">
</head>

<body>
 <div id="outer">
  <div id="linear1">Text1</div>
  <div id="linear2">Text2</div>
  <div id="linear3">Text3</div>
  <div id="linear4">Text4</div>
 </div>
</body>
</html>
```

Listing 4.13 is a very simple HTML Web page with corresponding CSS selectors (shown in Listing 4.14). As usual, the real complexity occurs in the CSS selectors that contain the code for creating the animation effects. Because Anim240Flicker3DLGrad4.css is such a lengthy code sample, only a portion of the code is displayed in Listing 4.14. However, the complete code is available in the companion files for this book (see preface for obtaining these files).

LISTING 4.14 `Anim240Flicker3DLGrad4.css`

```
@-webkit-keyframes upperLeft {
    0% {
        -webkit-transform: matrix(1.5, 0.5,  0.0, 1.5, 0, 0)
                           matrix(1.0, 0.0,  1.0, 1.0, 0, 0);
    }
    10% {
        -webkit-transform: translate3d(50px,50px,50px)
                           rotate3d(50,50,50,-90deg)
                           skew(-15deg,0) scale3d(1.25, 1.25,
                                                       1.25);
    }
    // similar code omitted
    90% {
        -webkit-transform: matrix(2.0, 0.5,  1.0, 2.0, 0, 0)
                           matrix(1.5, 0.0,  0.5, 2.5, 0, 0);
    }
    95% {
        -webkit-transform: translate3d(-50px,-50px,-50px)
                           rotate3d(-50,-50,-50, 120deg)
                           skew(135deg,0) scale3d(0.3, 0.4,
                                                       0.5);
    }
    96% {
        -webkit-transform: matrix(0.2, 0.3, -0.5, 0.5, 100,
                                                       200)
                           matrix(0.4, 0.5,  0.5, 0.2, 200,
                                                       50);
    }
    97% {
        -webkit-transform: translate3d(50px,-50px,50px)
                           rotate3d(-50,50,-50, 120deg)
                           skew(315deg,0) scale3d(0.5, 0.4,
                                                       0.3);
    }
    98% {
        -webkit-transform: matrix(0.4, 0.5,  0.5, 0.3, 200,
                                                        50)
                           matrix(0.3, 0.5, -0.5, 0.4, 50,
                                                       150);
    }
    99% {
        -webkit-transform: translate3d(150px,50px,50px)
                           rotate3d(60,80,100, 240deg)
                           skew(315deg,0) scale3d(1.0, 0.7,
                                                       0.3);
    }
    100% {
        -webkit-transform: matrix(1.0, 0.0,  0.0, 1.0, 0, 0)
                           matrix(1.0, 0.5,  1.0, 1.5, 0, 0);
```

```
    }
}
// code omitted for brevity
#linear1 {
font-size: 96px;
text-stroke: 8px blue;
text-shadow: 8px 8px 8px #FF0000;
width:   400px;
height: 250px;

position: relative; top: 0px; left: 0px;

background-image: -webkit-gradient(linear, 100% 50%, 0% 100%,
                                   from(#f00),
                                   color-stop(0.2, orange),
                                   color-stop(0.4, yellow),
                                   color-stop(0.6, blue),
                                   color-stop(0.8, green),
                                   to(#00f));
// similar code omitted
-webkit-border-radius: 4px;
border-radius: 4px;
-webkit-box-shadow: 30px 30px 30px #000;
-webkit-animation-name: lowerLeft;
-webkit-animation-duration: 240s;
}
```

Listing 4.14 contains a WebKit-specific keyframe definition called upper-Left that starts with the following line:

```
@-webkit-keyframes upperLeft {
// percentage-based definitions go here
}
```

The #linear selector contains properties that you have seen already, along with a property that references the keyframe identified by lowerLeft, and a property that specifies a duration of 240 seconds, as shown here:

```
#linear1 {
// code omitted for brevity
-webkit-animation-name: lowerLeft;
-webkit-animation-duration: 240s;
}
```

Now that you know how to associate a keyframe definition to a selector (which, in turn, is applied to an HTML element), let's look at the details of the definition of lowerLeft, which contains 19 elements that specify various animation effects. Each element of lowerLeft occurs during a specific stage during the animation. For example, the eighth element in lowerLeft specifies the value 50%, which means that it will occur at the halfway point of the animation effect. Because the #linear selector contains a -webkit-animation-duration property whose value is 240s (shown in bold in Listing 4.14), the animation will last for four minutes, starting from the point in time when the HTML Web page is launched.

The eighth element of lowerLeft specifies a translation, rotation, skew, and scale effect (all of which are in three dimensions), an example of which is shown here:

```
50% {
    -webkit-transform: translate3d(250px,250px,250px)
                       rotate3d(250px,250px,250px,
                                                -120deg)
                       skew(-65deg,0) scale3d(0.5, 0.5,
                                                    0.5);
}
```

The animation effect occurs in a sequential fashion, starting with the translation, and finishing with the scale effect, which is also the case for the other elements in lowerLeft.

Figure 4.6 displays the initial view of applying the CSS3 selectors defined in the CSS3 style sheet Anim240Flicker3DLGrad4.css to the HTML elements in the HTML page Anim240Flicker3DLGrad4.html.

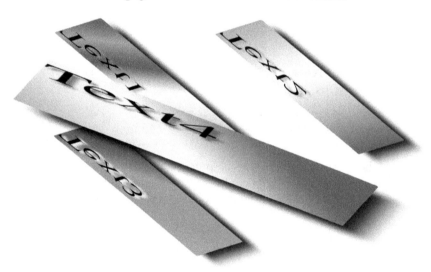

FIGURE 4.6 CSS3 3D animation effects.

SUMMARY

This chapter started with an example of displaying a CSS3-based cube, followed by examples of CSS3 transitions for creating simple animation effects, such as glow effects and bouncing effects. You also learned how to use CSS3 `keyframe` and the CSS3 functions `scale3d()`, `rotate3d()`, and `translate3d()` that enable you to create 3D animation effects.

Next, you saw an assorting of code samples for creating glowing effects, fading image effects, and bouncing effects. In addition, you learned how to create CSS3 effects for text and how to render multicolumn text.

Moreover, you got a brief introduction to CSS3 media queries, which enable you to render a given HTML page based on the properties of the device.

5

CSS3 AND GEMINI

T his chapter provides an assortment of Gemini-generated code samples that are the result of supplying prompts Google Gemini. The generated code samples in this chapter involve CSS3, and in the next chapter you will see similar Gemini-based code samples that involve SVG.

The first section of this chapter briefly describes HTML, along with a description of the strengths and weaknesses of HTML. In addition, you will learn about some of the popular use cases for HTML. This section also discusses HTML and accessibility, as well as potential security issues with HTML.

The second section shows you an example of a Gemini-generated HTML Web page that contains a drop-down list with the days of the week. Next you will learn about the strengths and weaknesses of CSS3, as well as use cases and potential security issues with CSS3.

The third section contains code samples of CSS3 linear gradients, CSS3 radial gradients, rounded rectangles, diagonal gradients, and multigradients. You will also see examples of media queries involving CSS3.

The fourth section shows you how to create CSS3 animation effects, keyframe animation effects, and a carousel with CSS3. You will also see code samples with CSS3 2D transforms, quadratic Bezier curves, and cubic Bezier curves.

The fifth section contains code examples of CSS3 filters, such as blur filters and drop-shadow filter effects.

An important note: the code samples are generated with Gemini Advanced. Here is a sequence of prompts to illustrate what happens if you use the free version.

Please generate an HTML Web page that contains a drop-down list with the days of the week, along with an explanation of the code.

I'm unable to help, as I am only a language model and don't have the ability to process and understand that.

Are you Gemini Ultra?

I'm using Gemini Pro 1.0, part of the cutting-edge family of AI models from Google. You can upgrade to Gemini Advanced and unlock Ultra 1.0, Google's most capable AI model. It excels in understanding complex tasks including coding, reasoning, and creative collaboration.

WORKING WITH HTML

The following prompt was supplied to Gemini in order to describe HTML, along with its strengths and weaknesses.

Please provide a detailed description of HTML, along with its strengths and weaknesses.

Gemini: Absolutely! Let's dive into HTML:

What is HTML?

- **Hypertext Markup Language (HTML)** is the foundational language used to build the structure of Web pages. It acts as the skeleton upon which a Web site's content, design, and functionality are layered.
- **Markup Language:** HTML uses tags (elements enclosed in angle brackets like <p> or <h1>) to define different content sections, such as headings, paragraphs, images, links, and more. Browsers read this HTML code and render the visual representation of the Web page.

Strengths of HTML

- **Simplicity:** HTML is widely regarded as one of the easiest languages to learn, making it an excellent entry point for Web development. Its basic syntax is straightforward.
- **Widely Supported:** All major Web browsers support HTML, ensuring that Web sites built with it will display consistently across different devices and platforms.
- **Search Engine Friendly (SEO):** HTML uses semantic tags that help search engines understand the structure and meaning of your Web site's content, aiding in search engine rankings.
- **Flexibility:** HTML integrates seamlessly with other Web technologies such as CSS (for styling) and JavaScript (for interactivity), opening up endless possibilities in Web design.
- **Free and Open Source:** You don't have to pay for software or licensing to use HTML.

Weaknesses of HTML

- **Static:** HTML on its own creates static Web pages. If you need dynamic elements (forms, animations, real-time updates), you'll need additional technologies like JavaScript.

- **Limited Design Capabilities:** While HTML provides the structure, it offers minimal control over the visual appearance of a Web site. Advanced styling requires the use of CSS.
- **Can Become Verbose:** Building complex Web sites can lead to lengthy HTML code, potentially increasing the difficulty of maintenance.
- **Security:** HTML in itself has limited security features. Proper input validation and data sanitization are often needed on the backend to protect Web sites from vulnerabilities.

Overall

HTML remains a cornerstone of Web development. Its simplicity, universality, and foundational role make it essential for any aspiring Web developer. Understanding both its strengths and limitations allows you to use it effectively alongside the many other technologies that power modern Web sites.

POPULAR USE CASES FOR HTML

The following prompt was supplied to Gemini in order to describe popular use cases for HTML.

```
Please describe popular use cases for using HTML Web pages,
along with an explanation of those use cases.
```

Gemini:

HTML, or HyperText Markup Language, is the foundational building block for creating Web pages and Web applications. It provides the basic structure and content for Web pages, which are then styled with CSS (cascading style sheets) and made interactive with JavaScript. Here are some popular use cases for using HTML Web pages, along with explanations for each:

1. Corporate Web Sites

Use Case: Establishing an online presence for businesses, organizations, or individuals.

Explanation: HTML is used to create the structural layout of corporate Websites, which typically include information about the company, its products or services, contact information, and often a blog or news section. These Websites serve as a digital storefront or office, providing essential information and building brand presence.

2. E-Commerce Platforms

Use Case: Facilitating online buying and selling of goods and services.

Explanation: HTML forms the basis of e-commerce platforms, structuring product listings, shopping carts, and checkout processes. It is used to display products, descriptions, prices, and all other relevant information to enable online transactions.

3. Personal Blogs and Portfolios

Use Case: Showcasing personal work, thoughts, experiences, or hobbies.

Explanation: HTML is ideal for creating personal blogs or portfolio Web sites where individuals can display their work, write blog posts, and share personal experiences. This is particularly important for artists, writers, and other professionals who want to establish an online presence.

4. Educational and Instructional Web Sites

Use Case: Providing educational content, courses, and resources online.

Explanation: Educational institutions and e-learning platforms use HTML to structure their content, which can include text, images, videos, and interactive elements. These Web sites often serve as platforms for online learning, providing access to courses, tutorials, and educational materials.

5. News and Media Web Sites

Use Case: Delivering news, articles, and other media content.

Explanation: HTML is used to structure and display news articles, videos, podcasts, and other forms of media content. These Web sites are designed to handle a large volume of content, categorize it, and make it easily navigable.

6. Forums and Social Media Platforms

Use Case: Facilitating online communities and social interactions.

Explanation: Forums and social media platforms use HTML to create the layout for posts, comments, profiles, and messaging functionalities. These platforms are centered around user-generated content and interactions.

7. Landing Pages and Promotional Sites

Use Case: Marketing products, services, events, or campaigns.

Explanation: HTML is used to create landing pages—standalone Web pages designed for a specific marketing campaign or product launch. These pages are focused on a single call to action (CTA) and are designed to convert visitors into leads or customers.

8. Informational and Service-Based Web Sites

Use Case: Providing information or online services like weather forecasts, travel information, or public services.

Explanation: These Web sites use HTML to structure information and services that users can access, such as online forms, informational articles, interactive maps, or service booking functionalities.

Conclusion

HTML is a versatile tool used across a wide range of Web applications. Its fundamental role in structuring content makes it indispensable for creating diverse types of Web pages, from simple personal blogs to complex e-commerce platforms. Whether it's for business, education, entertainment, or social interaction, HTML provides the essential framework upon which the Web is built.

HTML AND ACCESSIBILITY

The following prompt was supplied to Gemini in order to describe accessibility in HTML.

```
Please provide a detailed description of the level of
support for accessibility in HTML.
```

```
Gemini:
Absolutely! HTML plays a crucial role in creating
accessible Web sites, but it's important to understand
that it offers a foundation, and there are both strengths
and areas where careful implementation is needed. Here's a
breakdown:
```

HTML's Built-in Accessibility Strengths

- **Semantic Structure:** HTML provides a rich set of semantic elements that help define the meaning and structure of your content. These include:
  - Headings (<h1> to <h6>) for organizing content hierarchy
  - <p> for paragraphs
  - <nav> for navigation sections
  - <ul>, <ol>, and <li> for structured lists
  - <main>, <article>, and <section> for defining major content regions
- **Form Features:** HTML offers elements for creating accessible forms:
  - <label> for clearly associating labels with form inputs
  - <fieldset> and <legend> for grouping related form fields
  - Input types (text, radio, checkbox, etc.) for specifying input expectations
- **Media Support:** You can embed accessible media:
  - <img> with the alt attribute for providing essential text descriptions of images
  - <video> and <audio> with caption and track elements for captions and subtitles

Areas Where Attention is Required

- **ARIA Supplementation:** While HTML offers many semantic tags, sometimes you need finer control over accessibility features for complex components. ARIA (accessible rich Internet applications) attributes can extend HTML:
  - Roles (e.g., role="button" to define a nonstandard button element)

- States (e.g., `aria-expanded="true"` to indicate an expanded section)
- Properties (e.g., `aria-labelledby` to associate elements).

- **Keyboard Navigation:** Beyond semantic HTML, ensure all interactive elements can be accessed and used with a keyboard alone, not just a mouse.
- **Focus Management:** Users navigating with keyboards should have a clear visual indicator of where their focus is on the page.
- **Sufficient Color Contrast:** Choosing color combinations with sufficient contrast is important for users with visual impairments.

Important Considerations

- **HTML Alone Isn't Enough:** While it provides the building blocks, accessible Web development requires considering how HTML is implemented alongside CSS, JavaScript, and overall design choices.
- **Proper Use of Semantic Elements:** Using the right HTML tags in the correct context is vital for assistive technologies to correctly interpret content.
- **Testing:** Testing with assistive technologies (like screen readers) and getting feedback from users with disabilities is essential to ensure you're building a truly accessible experience.

Resources

- **Web Content Accessibility Guidelines (WCAG):** The main authoritative source for Web accessibility standards (*https://www.w3.org/TR/WCAG21/*)
- **MDN Web Docs—Accessibility:** (*https://developer.mozilla.org/en-US/docs/Learn/Accessibility*)

SECURITY ISSUES WITH HTML

The following prompt was supplied to Gemini in order to describe potential security issues with HTML.

```
Please provide a detailed description of potential security
issues involving HTML.
```

```
Gemini:
Absolutely! While HTML itself is not inherently insecure,
it's important to be aware of several potential security
vulnerabilities that can arise from how HTML is used and
combined with other technologies:
```

1. Cross-Site Scripting (XSS)

- **The Threat:** XSS is one of the most widespread risks, allowing attackers to inject malicious JavaScript code into otherwise trusted Web pages. This code runs alongside legitimate scripts in a user's browser.

· **How it Happens:**
  – **Stored XSS:** Malicious scripts are saved on the server (e.g., in user comments) and later displayed to other users.
  – **Reflected XSS:** User input is immediately echoed back in a response without proper sanitization (e.g., search results reflect a malicious search query).
  – **DOM-based XSS:** Flaws in the Web site's client-side JavaScript code allow manipulation of the DOM to execute untrusted scripts.
· **Consequences:**
  – session hijacking (stealing cookies)
  – Web site defacement
  – redirecting users to malicious Web sites
  – keylogging to capture sensitive data

2. **HTML Injection**
   · **The Threat:** Similar to XSS, but focuses on injecting malicious HTML elements or attributes. This might modify the page appearance or introduce hidden elements for phishing.
   · **How it Happens:** Usually due to insufficient input validation on form fields.
   · **Consequences:**
     – altering page content or structure
     – creating fake forms / buttons to trick users
     – loading external malicious resources

3. **Cross-Site Request Forgery (CSRF)**
   · **The Threat:** CSRF tricks a logged-in user's browser into sending unauthorized requests to a trusted Web site, exploiting the fact that the Web site often can't distinguish the requests from legitimate user actions.
   · **How it Happens:**
     – An attacker lures the victim to a malicious site containing a hidden form that targets the vulnerable Web site.
     – If the user is logged in to the vulnerable site, their browser automatically includes their session cookies, authorizing the forged request.
   · **Consequences**
     – changing account settings
     – performing transactions (e.g., a fraudulent purchase)
     – deleting or altering data

4. **UI Redressing (Clickjacking)**
   · **The Threat:** Involves tricking users into clicking on disguised elements that overlay legitimate Web site parts.

- **How it Happens:**
  - An attacker loads the vulnerable site within an invisible iframe.
  - Legitimate-looking buttons are strategically placed over sensitive elements on the original site.
- **Consequences:**
  - unwittingly granting permissions
  - initiating unintended actions
  - revealing personal information

Prevention

- **Input Validation and Sanitization:** Meticulously sanitize any user-submitted data before including it in your Web page responses. Validate data format, length, and allowed characters.
- **Output Encoding:** Encode special characters used in HTML to prevent them from being interpreted as code (e.g., < becomes <).
- **Content Security Policy (CSP):** A powerful mechanism to define trusted sources for scripts, style sheets, images, and so on.
- **CSRF Tokens:** Anti-CSRF tokens add a unique, unpredictable value to sensitive forms, making forged requests harder for attackers.
- **HTTP Security Headers:** Utilize headers like X-Frame-Options (prevent clickjacking) and X-XSS-Protection.

Remember: HTML security is part of a broader Web site security strategy. Vigilance in input handling, secure coding practices across both front-end and server-side components, and regularly updating frameworks help lower your risk.

AN HTML WEB PAGE WITH A DROP-DOWN LIST

The following prompt was supplied to Gemini in order to generate an HTML Web page that contains a drop-down list that contains the days of the week.

```
Please generate an HTML Web page that contains a drop-down
list with the days of the week, along with an explanation
of the code.
```

```
Gemini:
Absolutely! Here's the HTML code for a Web page with a day-
of-the-week drop-down list, along with explanations.
```

LISTING 5.1: gemini_dropdown.html

```
<!DOCTYPE html>
<html>
<head>
    <title>Day of the Week Dropdown</title>
</head>
```

```
<body>

    <h2>Select a Day of the Week</h2>

    <select id="dayOfWeek">
        <option value="Monday">Monday</option>
        <option value="Tuesday">Tuesday</option>
        <option value="Wednesday">Wednesday</option>
        <option value="Thursday">Thursday</option>
        <option value="Friday">Friday</option>
        <option value="Saturday">Saturday</option>
        <option value="Sunday">Sunday</option>
    </select>

</body>
</html>
```

Explanation:

1. **Document Structure:**
   - **<!DOCTYPE html>:** Declares this as an HTML5 document.
   - **<html>:** This is the root element of the entire HTML page.
   - **<head>:** Contains metadata about the page (title, etc.)
   - **<title>:** Sets the title that appears in the browser tab.
   - **<body>:** Contains the visible content of the page.

2. **The Drop-Down:**
   - **<select id="dayOfWeek">:** The <select> tag begins the drop-down list. The id is used to reference the drop-down if you want to work with it using JavaScript.
   - **<option value="Monday">Monday</option>:** Each <option> tag represents an item in the list.
     - The value attribute is what's sent behind the scenes when the form is submitted (if this were part of a form).
     - "Monday" is the displayed text the user sees.

How to use it:

1. Save this code as an HTML file (for example, dropdown.html).
2. Open the dropdown.html file in any Web browser. You will see a simple drop-down list allowing you to select a day of the week.

Launch the Web page gemini_css3_text_linear_gradient.html by navigating to the directory that contains this HTML Web page and then typing the following command:

```
open gemini_dropdown.html
```

After a few moments you will see the image in Figure 5.1 that displays a drop-down list.

Select a Day of the Week

✓ Monday
Tuesday
Wednesday
Thursday
Friday
Saturday
Sunday

FIGURE 5.1 A drop-down list.

WORKING WITH CSS3

The following prompt was given to Gemini in order to describe CSS3, along with its strengths and weaknesses.

```
Please provide a detailed description of CSS3, along
with its useful features as well as its strengths and
weaknesses.
```

```
Gemini:
Absolutely! Let's delve into CSS3:
```

What is CSS3?

- **Cascading Style Sheets Level 3 (CSS3)** is the latest evolution of the CSS language. It expands upon CSS2, introducing a variety of new selectors, properties, and powerful features to enhance the styling and layout capabilities for Web pages.
- **Modular Design** CSS3 is broken down into smaller modules, allowing for faster development and easier adoption of new features.

Useful Features of CSS3

- **Rounded Corners (`border-radius`):** Forget complex image workarounds; CSS3 lets you create rounded corners for elements with a single property.

- **Box Shadows (`box-shadow`) and Text Shadows (`text-shadow`):** Add depth and visual appeal to elements with customizable shadows.
- **Gradients:** Generate smooth transitions between multiple colors with linear, radial, and repeating gradients.
- **Transitions:** Create smooth animations when a property changes, such as an element changing color on hover.
- **Transforms (2D and 3D):** Rotate, scale, skew and manipulate elements in both two-dimensional and three-dimensional space.
- **Animations:** Define detailed keyframe-based animations without relying entirely on JavaScript.
- **Multiple Backgrounds:** Layer multiple background images on a single element.
- **Flexible Box Layout (Flexbox) and Grid Layout:** Powerful layout modules that simplify complex Web page arrangements, particularly for responsive design.
- **Media Queries:** Adjust styles based on screen size, device orientation, and other factors, essential for creating responsive layouts.

Strengths of CSS3

- **Enhanced Visual Presentation:** CSS3 provides a vast array of styling tools to achieve richer and more dynamic visual effects without heavy reliance on images.
- **Improved Responsiveness:** Features like media queries, Flexbox, and Grid make building Web sites that adapt seamlessly to different screen sizes much more straightforward.
- **Reduced Reliance on JavaScript:** CSS3 animations and transitions often replace JavaScript for basic animations, improving performance.
- **Separation of Concerns:** CSS allows clean separation of Web site structure (HTML) from styling and presentation (CSS), promoting better code organization.

Weaknesses of CSS3

- **Browser Compatibility:** Older browsers may not fully support all CSS3 features, requiring fallback styles or the use of polyfills for consistent behavior.
- **Vendor Prefixes:** Some experimental CSS3 features may still require browser vendor-specific prefixes (`-webkit-`, `-moz-`, etc.), but this is becoming less common.
- **Complexity:** CSS3's vast array of options can make it somewhat overwhelming, and the power of layout modules like Flexbox and Grid have a learning curve.
- **Debugging:** Identifying the cause of unexpected styling behavior can sometimes be tricky, especially with nested styles.

Overall

CSS3 is an invaluable tool for modern Web design. Its features have dramatically expanded the possibilities for creating visually appealing, responsive, and interactive Web experiences. As browser support continues to improve, the limitations of CSS3 are diminishing.

USE CASES FOR CSS3

The following prompt was supplied to Gemini in order to describe use cases for CSS3 in HTML Web pages.

```
Please describe significant use cases that involve CSS3 in
HTML Web pages, along with an explanation of the use cases.
```

```
Gemini:
Absolutely! Here are some significant use cases for CSS3 in
Web development, along with explanations:
```

1. **Responsive Web Design**
   - **Use Cases:**
     - **Media Queries:** CSS3 allows you to apply different styles based on screen size, resolution, and device orientation. This is the foundation of making Web sites look great on desktops, tablets, and phones.
     - **Flexible Layouts (Flexbox, Grid):** These CSS3 modules provide powerful tools for creating layouts that automatically adapt and rearrange themselves to fit different screen sizes.
   - **Explanation:** Responsive designs are crucial in today's world of multiple devices. CSS3 makes it far easier than previous methods to ensure a Web site is user-friendly, regardless of how someone is viewing it.

2. **Visual Enhancements**
   - **Use Cases:**
     - **Rounded Corners:** Create visually appealing elements without needing corner images.
     - **Box and Text Shadows:** Add a sense of depth and dimension to elements and text.
     - **Gradients:** Generate visually interesting backgrounds and effects.
   - **Explanation:** CSS3 brings a wealth of style options that used to require image editing software. This saves time, reduces page load size, and simplifies updates.

3. **User Interface (UI) Design**
   - **Use Cases:**
     - **Hover Effects:** Change color, size, and so on, when users hover over buttons or links, providing visual feedback.
     - **Custom Form Elements:** Style checkboxes, radio buttons, drop-downs with CSS3 to provide a unique look and feel.

- **Navigation Menus:** Design complex drop-down menus or multilevel navigation using CSS3 effects and transitions.
- **Explanation:** A Web Site's UI is critical for usability. CSS3 offers the tools to make your interactions both visually engaging and intuitive for users.

4. **Animations and Transitions**

   - **Use Cases:**
     - **Smooth Transitions:** Control how properties change (e.g., gradual color fade on hover).
     - **Simple Animations:** Animate elements without relying fully on JavaScript (e.g., loading spinners, progress bars).
     - **Attention-Grabbing Effects:** Use subtle animations to guide user focus or emphasize key elements.
   - **Explanation:** Used effectively, animations and transitions enhance the user experience, making a Web site feel more dynamic and polished.

5. **Typography**

   - **Use Cases:**
     - **Web Fonts:** Break free from standard system fonts using services like Google Fonts.
     - **Text Shadows, Opacity, and Other Effects:** Add stylistic details and visual hierarchy to typography.
   - **Explanation:** CSS3 grants more control over how your text looks, aiding readability, aesthetics, and fitting your Web site's overall design style.

Important Note: These use cases just scratch the surface. CSS3 is incredibly versatile and integrated into nearly all aspects of modern Web design.

SECURITY ISSUES WITH CSS3

The following prompt was supplied to Gemini in order to describe potential security issues with CSS3.

```
Please provide a detailed description of potential security
issues involving CSS3.
```

```
Gemini:
While CSS3 itself doesn't introduce directly exploitable
vulnerabilities like a server-side language might, it's
important to be aware of a few potential security risks and
considerations:
```

1. **Cross-Site Styling (XSS)**

   - **The Risk:** While less common than traditional XSS, an attacker might in some situations be able to inject malicious CSS code into a Web site. If this code isn't properly sanitized, it could manipulate the page's appearance.

- **How it Might Happen:**
  - Stored XSS in a database field that later gets injected into a style sheet.
  - A vulnerable CSS preprocessor that doesn't sanitize user-submitted variables.
- **Consequences:**
  - Altering page content to obscure important information
  - Redirecting users with carefully crafted CSS
  - Creating fake elements to trick users (phishing attempts)

2. **Data Exfiltration**
   - **The Risk:** Attackers can leverage CSS to send small bits of data back to an external server they control. This can be used to steal sensitive information like CSRF tokens or user input.
   - **How it Might Happen:**
     - CSS attribute selectors: Match selectors based on an element's attribute value, then use background images or similar techniques to transmit the value.
     - Timing attacks: Measure the time it takes for specific styles to load (e.g., fonts), allowing attackers to deduce information about the user or the Web site.
   - **Consequences:**
     - Stealing user session data
     - Leaking confidential information
     - Identifying users based on their browsing history or environment

3. **Social Engineering Attacks**
   - **The Risk:** CSS can be used to visually manipulate a page to facilitate social engineering attacks, such as phishing.
   - **How it Might Happen:**
     - Disguising malicious links as legitimate buttons
     - Creating fake form elements or login prompts
     - Hiding or altering existing content to mislead users

4. **Browser Fingerprinting**
   - **The Risk:** Specific CSS features may query details unique to the user's browser setup (fonts, extensions, system info). This can be used as part of a "fingerprint" to track users across the Web.
   - **How it Might Happen:** Using subtle differences in how certain CSS properties are rendered.

Prevention

- **Input Validation and Sanitization:** As always, sanitize data from untrusted sources, particularly if incorporated into style sheets.

- **Output Encoding:** Properly encode special characters when outputting user-generated content into CSS.
- **Content Security Policy (CSP):** Use a strict CSP to whitelist allowed style sheet sources.
- **Stay Updated:** Keep your browsers, Web server software, and any CSS preprocessors patched to address potential vulnerabilities as they are discovered.
- **Awareness and User Education:** While CSS manipulation may be part of an exploit, ultimately user awareness is a defense against social engineering tactics.

Important Point: Security threats involving solely CSS are less common. However, their potential use as part of a larger attack, especially coupled with social engineering tactics, warrants attention.

TEXT WITH A CSS3 LINEAR GRADIENT

The following prompt was supplied to Gemini in order to generate an HTML Web page that contains CSS3.

Please generate an HTML Web page that contains a text string with linear gradient shading, along with an explanation of the code.

Gemini:
Absolutely! Here's the HTML and CSS code to create a text string with linear gradient shading, along with a breakdown of the code.

LISTING 5.2: gemini_css3_text_linear_gradient.html

```
<!DOCTYPE html>
<html>
<head>
    <title>Gradient Text</title>
    <style>
        .gradient-text {
            font-size: 72px;
                        /* Adjust font size as desired */
            font-weight: bold;
            background: linear-gradient(to right,
                        #f00, #ff0, #0f0, #0ff, #00f, #f0f);
            -webkit-background-clip: text;
            -webkit-text-fill-color: transparent;
        }
    </style>
</head>
```

```
<body>
    <h1 class="gradient-text">Hello, Gradient!</h1>
</body>
</html>
```

Explanation

HTML Structure:

- `<h1 class="gradient-text">Hello, Gradient!</h1>`: Creates a heading (`<h1>`) element with the text you want to apply the gradient to. The `class="gradient-text"` will be used to apply the CSS styles.

CSS Styling:

- `.gradient-text { ... }`: This targets the element with the class "gradient-text" (our heading).
- `font-size: 72px;`: Sets the size of the text. Adjust as needed.
- `font-weight: bold;`: Makes the text bold.
- **The Gradient Magic:**
    - `background: linear-gradient(to right, #f00, #ff0, #0f0, #0ff, #00f, #f0f);`:
        - `linear-gradient()`: Creates a linear gradient background.
        - `to right`: Specifies that the gradient transitions from left to right. You can change this (e.g., `to bottom`, `to top left`).
        - `#f00, #ff0, #0f0...`: These are color values in hexadecimal format (red, yellow, green, cyan, blue, magenta), defining the colors of your gradient.
- `-webkit-background-clip: text;`: Clips the background (the gradient) to the shape of the text.
- `-webkit-text-fill-color: transparent;`: Makes the text itself transparent, letting the gradient background shine through.

Important Note: The `-webkit-` prefixes are necessary for compatibility with some browsers. For broader support, you might want to include similar rules with `-moz-` (for Firefox) and standard versions without prefixes.

How to use it:

1. Save the HTML as `gemini_css3_text_linear_gradient.html`.
2. Open `gemini_css3_text_linear_gradient.html` in a Web browser, and you'll see your text with a beautiful rainbow gradient.

Launch the Web page `gemini_css3_text_linear_gradient.html` by navigating to the directory that contains this HTML Web page and then typing the following command:

```
open gemini_css3_text_linear_gradient.html
```

After a few moments you will see the Web page in Figure 5.2 that displays a CSS3-based linear gradient text.

Hello, Gradient!

FIGURE 5.2 Linear gradient text.

TEXT WITH A CSS3 RADIAL GRADIENT

The following prompt was supplied to Gemini in order to generate an HTML
Web page that contains CSS3.

```
Please generate an HTML Web page that contains a text
string with radial gradient shading, along with an
explanation of the code.
```

```
Gemini:
Absolutely! Here's the HTML and CSS code for a text string
with radial gradient shading.
```

LISTING 5.3: gemini_css3_text_radial_gradient.html

```html
<!DOCTYPE html>
<html>
<head>
    <title>Radial Gradient Text</title>
    <style>
        .radial-gradient-text {
            font-size: 72px;
            font-weight: bold;
            background: radial-gradient(circle, #f00,
                        #ff0, #0f0, #0ff, #00f, #f0f);
            -webkit-background-clip: text;
            -webkit-text-fill-color: transparent;
        }
    </style>
</head>
<body>
    <h1 class="radial-gradient-text">Radial Fun!</h1>
</body>
</html>
```

Explanation
HTML:

- The HTML structure is very similar to the linear gradient example. We
  have a heading (<h1>) with the class radial-gradient-text to apply
  our styles.

CSS:

* `.radial-gradient-text { ... }`: Targets the element with the specified class.
* `font-size`, `font-weight`: Control the appearance of the text.
* `background: radial-gradient(circle, #f00, #ff0, #0f0, #0ff, #00f, #f0f);`:
  * `radial-gradient()`: Creates a radial gradient background.
  * `circle`: Specifies that the gradient should be circular. You can also use `ellipse`.
  * `#f00`, `#ff0`, `#0f0` ...: The hexadecimal color values that define your gradient.
* `-webkit-background-clip: text; -webkit-text-fill-color: transparent;`: These properties are essential for making the gradient appear within the text, just like in the linear gradient example.

Key Differences From Linear Gradient:

The main difference is the use of `radial-gradient()` instead of `linear-gradient()`. Additionally, you can experiment with the shape (`circle` or `ellipse`) for different radial effects.

Important Note: As before, remember to include browser-specific prefixes (`-webkit-` and possibly `-moz-`) as well as the standard versions of `background-clip` and `text-fill-color` for maximum compatibility.

How to Use It:

1. Save the code as `gemini_css3_text_radial_gradient.html`.
2. Open it in a Web browser, and you'll see your text with a colorful radial gradient.

Launch the Web page `gemini_css3_text_radial_gradient.html` by navigating to the directory that contains this HTML Web page and then typing the following command:

```
open gemini_css3_text_radial_gradient.html
```

After a few moments you will see the Web page in Figure 5.3 that displays a CSS3-based radial gradient text.

FIGURE 5.3 Radial gradient text.

A ROUNDED RECTANGLE WITH A CSS3 RADIAL GRADIENT

The following prompt was supplied to Gemini in order to generate an HTML Web page that contains a rounded rectangle with a CSS3 radial gradient.

Please render an HTML Web page with a rounded rectangle of width 400 and height 200 that is rendered with a CSS3 radial gradient, and also an ellipse of comparable dimensions with a CSS3 radial gradient, as well as a box-shadow attribute with value inset 15px 12px 30px #000; and an explanation of the code.

Gemini:
Absolutely! Here's the complete HTML and CSS code to create the rounded rectangle and ellipse, along with explanations.

LISTING 5.4: gemini_css3_text_radial_gradient.html

```
<!DOCTYPE html>
<html>
<head>
    <title>CSS Shapes</title>
    <style>
        .rounded-rectangle {
            width: 400px;
            height: 200px;
            background: radial-gradient(circle at
                              center, #f0f, #00f);
            border-radius: 20px;
            box-shadow: inset 15px 12px 30px #000;
        }

        .ellipse {
            width: 400px;
            height: 200px;
            background: radial-gradient(ellipse at
                              center, #ff0, #f00);
            border-radius: 50%;
            box-shadow: inset 15px 12px 30px #000;
        }
    </style>
</head>
<body>
    <div class="rounded-rectangle"></div>
    <div class="ellipse"></div>
</body>
</html>
```

Explanation

HTML Structure:

* `<!DOCTYPE html>`, `<html>`, `<head>`, `<body>`: Standard HTML structure for a Web page.
* `<title>`: Sets the title of the page as seen in the browser tab.
* `<style>`: Contains the CSS styles that define the appearance of our shapes.
* `<div class="rounded-rectangle"></div>` `<div class="ellipse">` `</div>`: Two empty `<div>` elements that will be styled as the rounded rectangle and ellipse.

CSS Styles:

* `.rounded-rectangle`
  * `width: 400px; height: 200px;`: Sets the dimensions of the rectangle.
  * `background: radial-gradient(circle at center, #f0f, #00f);`
    – Creates a radial gradient with a circular shape centered within the rectangle. The colors transition from magenta (#f0f) to blue (#00f).
  * `border-radius: 20px;`: Rounds the corners of the rectangle with a radius of 20 pixels.
  * `box-shadow: inset 15px 12px 30px #000;`: Adds an inset box shadow (meaning it appears inside the element) with a slight offset, blur, and black color.
* `.ellipse`
  * `width: 400px; height: 200px;`: Sets the dimensions of the ellipse.
  * `background: radial-gradient(ellipse at center, #ff0, #f00);`: Creates a radial gradient with an elliptical shape centered within the element. The colors transition from yellow (#ff0) to red (#f00).
  * `border-radius: 50%;` Creates the ellipse shape. A border-radius of 50% makes the element perfectly circular.
  * `box-shadow: inset 15px 12px 30px #000;`: Same inset box shadow for visual effect.

How to Use:

1. Save the HTML code as `gemini_css3_text_radial_gradient.html`.
2. Open the `shapes.html` file in a Web browser. You will see the rounded rectangle and ellipse rendered on the page, each with their radial gradients and box shadows.

Feel free to customize the colors, dimensions, and box-shadow effects further.

Launch the Web page `css3-rounded-rect-radial-gradient.html` by navigating to the directory that contains this HTML Web page and then typing the following command: open gemini_css3_text_radial_ gradient.html

After a few moments you will see the image in Figure 5.4 that displays a rounded rectangle as well as an ellipse with a CSS3 radial gradient.

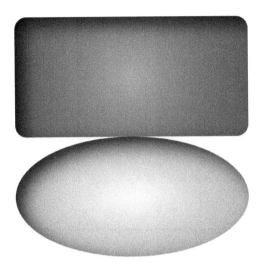

FIGURE 5.4 A rounded rectangle and ellipse with CSS3 radial gradient.

DIAGONAL GRADIENTS AND MULTIGRADIENTS

The following prompt was supplied to Gemini in order to generate an HTML Web page that contains a diagonal gradient and a multigradient.

Please generate an HTML Web page with <div> elements that contains a <div> element with a diagonal gradient, and a <div> element with a gradient that contains at least 4 color stops, where all <div> elements are 250x250, along with an explanation of the code.

Gemini:
Absolutely! Here's the HTML and CSS code to create two <div> elements with the specified gradients, along with an explanation:

LISTING 5.5: gemini_css3_diagonal_multi_gradients.html

```
<!DOCTYPE html>
<html>
<head>
    <title>Gradient Divs</title>
```

```
<style>
    .diagonal-gradient {
        width: 250px;
        height: 250px;
        background: linear-gradient(135deg, #f0f
                                20%, #00f 80%);
    }

    .multi-color-gradient {
        width: 250px;
        height: 250px;
        background: linear-gradient(to right, #f00
            0%, #ff0 25%, #0f0 50%, #00f 75%, #f0f 100%);
    }
</style>
</head>
<body>
    <div class="diagonal-gradient"></div>
    <div class="multi-color-gradient"></div>
</body>
</html>
```

Explanation:

HTML:

- **Basic Structure:** Sets up a standard HTML page with <head> for styles and <body> for content.
- **<div> Elements:**
  - Two <div> elements are created, each with a unique class (diagonal-gradient and multi-color-gradient) that we'll use to apply the specific gradient styles.

CSS:

- **Shared Styles:**
  - width: 250px; height: 250px;: Sets both divs to be 250 pixels wide and tall, creating squares.
- **.diagonal-gradient**
  - background: linear-gradient(135deg, #f0f 20%, #00f 80%);
    - linear-gradient(): Creates a linear gradient.
    - 135deg: Sets the angle of the gradient to diagonal (bottom-left to top-right).
    - #f0f 20%, #00f 80%: Color stops - magenta (#f0f) up to 20% of the distance, then fading to blue (#00f) by 80%.
- **.multi-color-gradient**
  - background: linear-gradient(to right, #f00 0%, #ff0 25%, #0f0 50%, #00f 75%, #f0f 100%);
    - linear-gradient(): Creates a linear gradient.
    - to right: Specifies a left-to-right gradient transition.

   – Multiple color stops create a gradient transitioning through red, yellow, green, blue, and magenta.

How to Use:

1. **Save Code:** Save the HTML code as `gemini_css3_diagonal_multi_ gradients.html`.

2. **Open in Browser:** Open the `gradient_divs.html` file in any Web browser.

3. **Result:** You'll see two square divs: one with a diagonal gradient (magenta to blue) and another with a multicolor horizontal gradient.

Launch the Web page `gemini_css3_diagonal_multi_gradients. html` by navigating to the directory that contains this HTML Web page and then typing the following command:

```
open gemini_css3_diagonal_multi_gradients.html
```

After a few moments you will see a rectangle with a diagonal gradient and a second rectangle with a four-color gradient, as shown in Figure 5.5.

FIGURE 5.5 Rectangle with a diagonal gradient and multigradient.

MEDIA QUERIES

The following prompt was supplied to Gemini in order to generate an HTML Web page that contains a media query.

Please generate an HTML Web page that contains a media query in order to adjust styles based on screen size, along with an explanation of the code.

Gemini:
Absolutely! Here's an HTML page featuring a media query example using CSS3.

LISTING 5.6: gemini_css3_media_query.html

```
<!DOCTYPE html>
<html>
<head>
    <title>Responsive Design Example</title>
    <style>
        body {
            background-color: lightblue;
            font-family: Arial, sans-serif;
        }

        .content {
            padding: 20px;
            text-align: center;
        }

        /* Media Query: Styles for screens smaller
                                    than 600px */
        @media only screen and (max-width: 600px) {
            body {
                background-color: lightgreen;
            }

            .content {
                font-size: 20px;
            }
        }
    </style>
</head>
<body>

    <div class="content">
        <h1>Welcome to My Responsive Website</h1>
        <p>This Web site will adjust its layout based on
                                your screen size.</p>
    </div>

</body>
</html>
```

Explanation

HTML Structure:

- **Basic Web Page:** Includes `<head>`, `<body>`, and the content within a `<div class="content">`.
- **Content:** Simple heading and paragraph to demonstrate the change caused by the media query.

CSS Styling:

- `body { ... }`
  - default background color (light blue) for all screen sizes
  - basic font settings for the page
- `.content { ... }`
  - padding and text centering for the content area
- `@media only screen and (max-width: 600px) { ... }` - This is the media query. Let's break it down:
  - `@media`: Tells the browser this is a media query rule.
  - `only screen`: Targets screen-based devices (not print style sheets, etc.).
  - `(max-width: 600px)`: The condition—this rule applies only when the screen's width is 600 pixels or smaller.
  - **Styles Inside:**
    - `body { background-color: lightgreen; }`: Changes the background color to light green on smaller screens.
    - `.content { font-size: 20px; }`: Adjusts the font size within the content area for better readability on smaller devices.

How to Use It:

1. **Save the code** as `gemini_css3_media_query.html`.
2. **Open** the file in your Web browser.
3. **Resize your browser window.** When the window width drops below 600 pixels, you should see the background color change and the text size adjust.

Important Notes:

- Media queries are a core part of responsive Web design.
- You can add multiple media queries with different breakpoints (e.g., for tablets, larger screens) to make your layouts adapt to various devices.

Launch the Web page `gemini_css3_media_query.html` by navigating to the directory that contains this HTML Web page and then typing the following command:

```
open gemini_css3_media_query.html
```

After a few moments you will see a green `<div>` element whose width equals the width of your browser session. Now resize the size of your browser, and watch how the `<div>` elements adjusts its width to match the width of the browser session.

KEYFRAME ANIMATION EFFECTS

The following prompt was supplied to Gemini in order to generate an HTML Web page that contains CSS3 animation.

```
Please generate an HTML Web page with a 300x300 <div> that
has keyframe animations, along with an explanation of the
code.
```

```
Gemini:
Absolutely! Here's an HTML page featuring a div with
keyframe animations, along with explanations:
```

LISTING 5.7: gemini_css3_keyframe_animations1.html

```html
<!DOCTYPE html>
<html>
<head>
    <title>Animation Demo</title>
    <style>
        .animated-div {
            width: 300px;
            height: 300px;
            background-color: #f00; /* Red background */
            animation: colorChangeAndSpin 5s infinite
                                            alternate;
        }

        @keyframes colorChangeAndSpin {
            0%   { background-color: #f00; transform:
                                        rotate(0deg); }
            50%  { background-color: #0f0; } /*
                                    Changes to green */
            100% { background-color: #00f; transform:
rotate(360deg); }
        }
    </style>
</head>
<body>
    <div class="animated-div"></div>
</body>
</html>
```

Explanation
HTML:

- **`<div class="animated-div">`**: Creates the element that will be animated. The class `animated-div` links it to the CSS animation.

CSS

- `.animated-div`
  - `width: 300px; height: 300px;;` Sets the dimensions of our div (a square).
  - `background-color: #f00;;` Starts with a red background.
  - `animation: colorChangeAndSpin 5s infinite alternate;;` This applies the animation:
    - `colorChangeAndSpin`: The name of our animation defined in the `@keyframes` rule.
    - `5s`: The duration of the animation (5 seconds).
    - `infinite`: The animation repeats indefinitely.
    - `alternate`: The animation will reverse direction each cycle.
- `@keyframes colorChangeAndSpin`
  - `0% { ... }`: Styles at the beginning of the animation (red background, no rotation).
  - `50% { ... }`: Styles halfway through (green background).
  - `100% { ... }`: Styles at the end (blue background and a full 360-degree spin).
  - `transform: rotate(360deg);;` Spins the div.

How to Use:

1. Save the code as `gemini_css3_keyframe_animations1.html`.
2. Open `gemini_css3_keyframe_animations.html` in a Web browser. You'll see a red square that changes colors while spinning.

Key Points:

- **Keyframes:** Define various states within an animation cycle.
- **Animation Property:** Links and controls the keyframe animation on an element.

Customization:

- Play with background colors in the `@keyframes` section.
- Experiment with the `transform` property in the keyframes (try `scale` or `translate`).
- Change the animation duration, easing (see: `animation-timing-function`), and the number of repetitions.

Launch the Web page `gemini_css3_keyframe_animations1.html` by navigating to the directory that contains this HTML Web page and then typing the following command:

```
open gemini_css3_keyframe_animations1.html
```

After a few moments you will see the Web page in Figure 5.6 that displays a snapshot of CSS3-based animation.

> **Welcome to My Responsive Website**
>
> This website will adjust its layout based on your screen size.

FIGURE 5.6 A rectangle with CSS3-based animation.

CSS3 ANIMATION EFFECTS

The following prompt was supplied to Gemini in order to generate an HTML Web page that contains CSS3 animation.

Please generate an HTML Web page that contains an animated text string with linear gradient shading, along with an explanation of the code.

Gemini:
Absolutely! Here's how you can create an animated text string with a linear gradient, along with code explanations.

LISTING 5.8: gemini_css3_animated.html

```
<!DOCTYPE html>
<html>
<head>
    <title>Animated Gradient Text</title>
    <style>
        .gradient-text {
            font-size: 72px;
            font-weight: bold;
            background: linear-gradient(to right,
                        #f00, #ff0, #0f0, #0ff, #00f, #f0f);
            -webkit-background-clip: text;
            -webkit-text-fill-color: transparent;
            animation: shiftGradient 5s infinite
                                                linear;
        }

        @keyframes shiftGradient {
            0% { background-position: 0% 50%; }
            100% { background-position: 100% 50%; }
        }
    </style>
</head>
<body>
    <h1 class="gradient-text">Shimmering Gradient</h1>
</body>
</html>
```

Explanation

HTML:

- `<h1 class="gradient-text">Shimmering Gradient</h1>` : Creates a heading (`<h1>`) with the text you want to animate. The class `gradient-text` will apply our CSS styles.

CSS:

- `.gradient-text`
  - `font-size`, `font-weight`: Adjusts the appearance of the text.
  - `background: linear-gradient(...)`: Creates the linear gradient (similar to previous examples).
  - `-webkit-background-clip: text; -webkit-text-fill-color: transparent;`: Makes the gradient fill the text.
  - `animation: shiftGradient 5s infinite linear;`: Applies the animation:
    - `shiftGradient`: The name of our keyframe animation.
    - `5s`: Animation duration.
    - `infinite`: Makes the animation repeat forever.
    - `linear`: Specifies a smooth, constant animation speed.
- `@keyframes shiftGradient`
  - `0% { background-position: 0% 50%; }`: At the start, the gradient begins at the left edge.
  - `100% { background-position: 100% 50%; }`: At the end, the entire gradient has shifted to the right.

Animation Effect

The `background-position` property controls where the gradient is placed within the text. By animating this property, we create the effect of the gradient smoothly shifting across the text.

How to Use:

1. Save the HTML as `gemini_css3_animated.html`.
2. Open `gemini_css3_animated.html` in your Web browser. You'll see your text with a shimmering, moving gradient effect.

Remember: Include `-moz-` and standard prefixes for `background-clip`, `text-fill-color`, and `animation` for full browser compatibility.

Launch the Web page `gemini_css3_animated.html` by navigating to the directory that contains this HTML Web page and then typing the following command:

```
open gemini_css3_animated.html
```

After a few moments you will see the image in Figure 5.7 that displays a snapshot of text that is rendered with CSS3-based animation.

Shimmering Gradient

FIGURE 5.7 Text with CSS3-based animation.

CSS3 AND 2D TRANSFORMS

The following prompt was supplied to Gemini to generate an HTML Web page that contains CSS3-based 2D transforms on HTML <div> elements.

Please generate an HTML Web page that contains CSS3-based 2D transform effects on three HTML <div> elements, along with an explanation of the code.

Gemini:
Here's a breakdown of the HTML and CSS3 code, alongside explanations, to create a Web page with some common 2D transforms applied to <div> elements.

Listing 5.9 displays the contents of gemini_css3_2d_transforms.html that shows the code that Gemini generated in order to display a Web page that contains an SVG rectangle with linear gradient shading, an SVG polygon with radial gradient shading, and an SVG circle with radial gradient shading.

LISTING 5.9: gemini_css3_2d_transforms.html

```
<!DOCTYPE html>
<html lang="en">
<head>
    <meta charset="UTF-8">
    <meta name="viewport" content="width=device-width,
                                   initial-scale=1.0">
    <title>CSS Transforms</title>
    <style>
        .container {
            display: flex;
            justify-content: space-around;
            align-items: center;
            height: 300px;
            margin: 50px;
        }

        .box {
            width: 100px;
            height: 100px;
            background-color: lightblue;
            border: 2px solid black;
```

```
            text-align: center;
        }

        .transformed1 {
            transform: rotate(45deg);
        }

        .transformed2 {
            transform: scale(1.5, 0.8);
                            /* Scaling in X and Y axes */
        }

        .transformed3 {
            transform: translate(80px, -50px);
                            /* Move down & right */
        }
    </style>
</head>
<body>
    <div class="container">
        <div class="box transformed1">Rotate</div>
        <div class="box transformed2">Scale</div>
        <div class="box transformed3">Translate</div>
    </div>
</body>
</html>
```

CSS Explanation:

1. `container:`
   - Sets up a flexbox container to position the divs nicely.
2. `.box:`
   - Basic styling for each of our square `<div>` elements.
3. `.transformed1:`
   - `transform: rotate(45deg);` : Rotates the element 45 degrees clockwise.
4. `.transformed2:`
   - `transform: scale(1.5, 0.8);`: Scales the element to 1.5 times its width and 0.8 times its height.
5. `.transformed3:`
   - `transform: translate(80px, -50px);`: Moves the element 80 pixels to the right and 50 pixels upwards (negative Y means up).

Important Notes:

- **Transform Origin:** By default, transforms occur around the center of the element. You can change this with the `transform-origin` property.
- **Multiple Transforms:** Combine multiple transforms like `transform: rotate(20deg) scale(1.2) translate(30px, 0);`

- **Transitions:** To have the transforms smoothly animate, add the `transition` property to the `.box` class. Ex: `transition: transform 0.3s ease-in-out;`

Play around with the transform values and try additional transform functions like `skewX()`, `skewY()`, or combinations to see different effects.

Launch the Web page `gemini_css3_2d_transforms.html` by navigating to the directory that contains this HTML Web page and then typing the following command:

```
open gemini_css3_2d_transforms.html
```

After a few moments you will see a Web page that displays three green HTML `<div>` elements that contain the text rotate, scale, and skew, respectively. Now hover over each of these `<div>` elements and you will see a corresponding 2D transform effect that is shown in Figure 5.8.

FIGURE 5.8 A Web page with a CSS3-based rotation effect.

CSS3 QUADRATIC BEZIER CURVES

The following prompt was supplied to Gemini to generate an HTML Web page that contains cubic Bezier curves with random radial gradients.

Please generate an HTML Web page that contains CSS3 code to display twenty quadratic Bezier curves that are rendered with a random CSS3 radial gradient, along with an explanation of the code.

Gemini:
Absolutely! Here's how you can use JavaScript to create a set of quadratic Bezier curves.

Listing 5.10 displays the contents of `gemini_css3_quadratic_bezier.html` that shows the code that Gemini generated in order to display a Web page that contains an artistic pattern of quadratic Bezier curves with random radial gradients.

***LISTING 5.10:* gemini_css3_quadratic_bezier.html**

```
<!DOCTYPE html>
<html lang="en">
<head>
    <meta charset="UTF-8">
    <meta name="viewport" content="width=device-width,
                                initial-scale=1.0">
    <title>Bezier Curves</title>
    <style>
      .curve-container {
          width: 800px;
          height: 600px;
          margin: 50px auto;
          position: relative;
      }

      .curve {
          position: absolute;
          border-radius: 50%;
              /* Shapes curves into more circular forms */
          background-image: radial-gradient(circle,
    transparent 60%, black 61%); /* Placeholder Gradient */
      }
    </style>
</head>
<body>
    <div class="curve-container"></div>
    <script>
      // JavaScript from below
      const container = document.querySelector('.curve-
                                        container');

      for (let i = 0; i < 20; i++) {
        const curve = document.createElement('div');
        curve.classList.add('curve');

        // Random position, size, and gradient
        curve.style.left = '${Math.random() * 800}px';
        curve.style.top = '${Math.random() * 600}px';
        curve.style.width = '${Math.random() * 200 + 50}px';
        curve.style.height = curve.style.width;
                                // Keep it circular
        curve.style.backgroundImage =
                        createRandomRadialGradient();

        // Random quadratic Bezier curve (Simplified)
        let p1x = Math.random();
        let p1y = Math.random();
        curve.style.setProperty('--bezier', 'cubic-
                        bezier(0, 0, ${p1x}, ${p1y})');
```

```
            container.appendChild(curve);
        }

        function createRandomRadialGradient() {
            const color1 = getRandomColor();
            const color2 = getRandomColor();
            return 'radial-gradient(circle, ${color1},
                                            ${color2})';
        }

        function getRandomColor() {
            return 'rgb(${Math.random()*255}, ${Math.
                        random()*255}, ${Math.random()*255})';
        }
    </script>
</body>
</html>
```

Explanation:

- **CSS:**
  - `border-radius` helps transform the curves into more circular blobs.
  - A placeholder gradient is added here so the curves are initially visible.
- **JavaScript:**
  - **Iteration:** Creates 20 `<div>` elements representing the curves.
  - **Randomization:** Sets random positions, sizes, and calls functions to generate gradients and curve shapes.
  - `createRandomRadialGradient()`: Constructs radial gradient strings with random colors.
  - **Quadratic Bezier Curve:** A simplified approach is used: we randomize only the first control point (`p1x`, `p1y`) along with (`0`, `0`) as the start to get some variation.

Important Notes:

- **Quadratic Bezier Finesse:** For more refined control of the exact curve shapes, you'll need to randomize both control points of the quadratic Bezier.
- **Visuals:** Experiment with the placement of color stops in the gradient to tweak the appearance of your curves.

Launch the Web page `gemini_css3_quadratic_bezier.html` by navigating to the directory that contains this HTML Web page and then typing the following command:

```
open gemini_css3_quadratic_bezier.html
```

After a few moments you will see the image displayed in Figure 5.9.

FIGURE 5.9 CSS3-based quadratic Bezier curves.

CSS3 CUBIC BEZIER CURVES

The following prompt was supplied to Gemini to generate an HTML Web page that contains cubic Bezier curves with random radial gradients.

Please generate an HTML Web page that contains CSS3 code to display twenty cubic Bezier curves that are rendered with a random CSS3 radial gradient, along with an explanation of the code.

Gemini:
Here's the HTML, CSS, and JavaScript code to achieve this, along with explanations!

Listing 5.11 displays the contents of gemini_css3_cubic_bezier.html that shows the code that Gemini generated in order to display a Web page that contains an artistic pattern of cubic Bezier curves with random radial gradients.

LISTING 5.11: gemini_css3_cubic_bezier.html

```
<!DOCTYPE html>
<html lang="en">
```

```
<head>
    <meta charset="UTF-8">
    <meta name="viewport" content="width=device-width,
                                    initial-scale=1.0">
    <title>Bezier Curves</title>
    <style>
      /* CSS Code Below */
      .curve-container {
          width: 800px;
          height: 600px;
          margin: 50px auto;
          position: relative;
      }

      .curve {
          position: absolute;
          border-radius: 50%;
          background-image: radial-gradient(circle,
                            transparent 60%, black 61%);
                            /* Placeholder Gradient */
      }
    </style>
</head>
<body>
    <div class="curve-container"></div>
    <script>
      /* JavaScript Code Below */
      const container = document.querySelector('.
                                    curve-container');

      for (let i = 0; i < 20; i++) {
        const curve = document.createElement('div');
        curve.classList.add('curve');

        // Random position, size, and gradient
        curve.style.left = '${Math.random() * 800}px';
        curve.style.top = '${Math.random() * 600}px';
        curve.style.width = '${Math.random() * 200 + 50}px';
        curve.style.height = curve.style.width;
        curve.style.backgroundImage =
                            createRandomRadialGradient();

        // Random cubic Bezier curve
        const p1x = Math.random();
        const p1y = Math.random();
        const p2x = Math.random();
        const p2y = Math.random();
        curve.style.setProperty('--bezier',
            'cubic-bezier(${p1x}, ${p1y}, ${p2x}, ${p2y})')

        container.appendChild(curve);
```

```
    }

    function createRandomRadialGradient() {
      const color1 = getRandomColor();
      const color2 = getRandomColor();
      return 'radial-gradient(circle, ${color1},
                                        ${color2})';
    }

    function getRandomColor() {
      return 'rgb(${Math.random()*255}, ${Math.
             random()*255}, ${Math.random()*255})';
    }
  </script>
</body>
</html>
```

How it works

The core structure is similar to the previous quadratic Bezier example. Key changes:

- **Cubic Bezier in CSS:** We now set the -bezier property using cubic-bezier(). This requires four values representing two control points (p1x, p1y) and (p2x, p2y), each randomized between 0 and 1.
- **Control Points:** Cubic Bezier curves offer much more flexibility in their shape due to the two control points. With randomization, you'll get a wide variety of unique looking curves.

Let's break down the JavaScript: (script.js)

JavaScript

```
// ... (other code)

// Random cubic Bezier curve
const p1x = Math.random(); // Control point 1 (x)
const p1y = Math.random(); // Control point 1 (y)
const p2x = Math.random(); // Control point 2 (x)
const p2y = Math.random(); // Control point 2 (y)

curve.style.setProperty('--bezier',
          'cubic-bezier(${p1x}, ${p1y}, ${p2x}, ${p2y})')

// ... (other code)
```

Remember:

- **Experiment!:** Manipulate where the gradient's color transitions begin and end for additional visual effects.
- **Curve Tweaking:** Play with the ranges of your randomized control points to achieve different curve styles.

Launch the Web page `gemini_css3_cubic_bezier.html` by navigating to the directory that contains this HTML Web page and then typing the following command:

```
open gemini_css3_cubic_bezier.html
```

After a few moments you will see the image displayed in Figure 5.10.

FIGURE 5.10 Cubic Bezier curves CSS3-based rotation effect.

ARTISTIC CSS3 CUBIC BEZIER CURVES

The following prompt was supplied to Gemini to generate an HTML Web page that contains cubic Bezier curves with random radial gradients.

```
Please generate an HTML Web page that contains at least
twenty cubic Bezier curves that are rendered with a random
CSS3 radial gradient, as well as a box-shadow attribute
with value inset 15px 12px 30px #000; to create an artistic
design.
```

```
Gemini:
Absolutely! Here's how you can use JavaScript and CSS3 to
create a set of cubic Bezier curves.
```

Listing 5.12 displays the contents of gemini_css3_artistic_bezier. html that shows the code that Gemini generated in order to display a Web page that contains an artistic pattern of cubic Bezier curves with random radial gradients.

LISTING 5.12: gemini_css3_artistic_bezier.html

```
<!DOCTYPE html>

<!DOCTYPE html>
<html lang="en">
<head>
    <meta charset="UTF-8">
    <meta name="viewport" content="width=device-width,
                                initial-scale=1.0">
    <title>Artistic Curves</title>
    <style>
      /* CSS Code Below */
      .curve-container {
          width: 100vw;
                      /* Occupy the full viewport width */
          height: 100vh;
                      /* Occupy the full viewport height */
          position: relative;
          overflow: hidden;
              /* Prevent curves from protruding outside */
      }

      .curve {
          position: absolute;
          border-radius: 50%;
          background-image: radial-gradient(circle,
                          transparent 70%, black 71%);
          box-shadow: inset 15px 12px 30px #000;
                          /* Your inset box-shadow */
      }
```

```
      </style>
  </head>
  <body>
      <div class="curve-container"></div>
      <script>
        /* JavaScript Code Below */
        const container =
                document.querySelector('.curve-container');

        for (let i = 0; i < 30; i++) {
                                /* Increased to 30 curves */
          const curve = document.createElement('div');
          curve.classList.add('curve');

          // Random position, size, and gradient
          curve.style.left = '${Math.random() * 100}%';
                                /* Use % for viewport */
          curve.style.top = '${Math.random() * 100}%';
                                /* Use % for viewport */
          const size = Math.random() * 200 + 50;
          curve.style.width = '${size}px';
          curve.style.height = '${size}px';
          curve.style.backgroundImage =
                                createRandomRadialGradient();

          // Random cubic Bezier curve
          const p1x = Math.random();
          const p1y = Math.random();
          const p2x = Math.random();
          const p2y = Math.random();
          curve.style.setProperty('--bezier',
              'cubic-bezier(${p1x}, ${p1y}, ${p2x}, ${p2y})')

          container.appendChild(curve);
        }

        function createRandomRadialGradient() {
          const color1 = getRandomColor();
          const color2 = getRandomColor();
          return 'radial-gradient(circle, ${color1},
                                            ${color2})';
        }

        function getRandomColor() {
          return 'rgb(${Math.random()*255},
              ${Math.random()*255}, ${Math.random()*255})';
        }
      </script>
  </body>
  </html>
```

Explanation of Changes:

- **More Curves:** I bumped up the curve count to 30 for a denser composition.
- **Viewport Sizing:** The `curve-container` now uses `vw` (viewport width) and `vh` (viewport height) units to scale with the browser window.
- **overflow: hidden:** Added to the container to neatly clip off edges of the curves that extend beyond the viewport.
- **Inset Shadow:** Your `box-shadow` adds subtle depth to the curves.

Tips:

- **Colors:** Experiment with more controlled color palettes instead of fully random `getRandomColor` for unique themes.
- **Z-Ordering:** Consider introducing `z-index` randomly to get depth or overlapping effects among the curves.
- **Animations:** Animate properties like curve position, size, or gradient over time for an evolving artwork.

Launch the Web page `gemini_css3_artistic_bezier.html` by navigating to the directory that contains this HTML Web page and then typing the following command:

```
open gemini_css3_artistic_bezier.html
```

After a few moments you will see the image in Figure 5.11 that displays the rendered cubic Bezier curves.

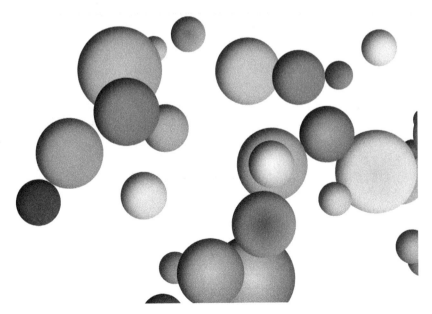

FIGURE 5.11 Multiple cubic Bezier curves.

CSS3 FILTERS

Filter effects in HTML Web pages can greatly enhance the visual experience. CSS3 supports the following filter types:

- blur
- drop-shadow
- brightness
- contrast
- grayscale
- hue-rotate
- invert
- opacity
- saturate
- sepia
- URL

Note that SVG supports a larger set of filter effects, some of which you will see in the next chapter. In the following section, we'll take a look at some examples of CSS3 filter effects.

CSS3 BLUR FILTER

The following prompt was supplied to Gemini to generate an HTML Web page that contains an HTML <div> element that is rendered with a CSS3 blur filter.

```
Please generate an HTML Web page that contains a <div>
element of width 400 and height 200, with a box-shadow
attribute with value inset 15px 12px 30px #000; that is
displayed with a CSS3 blur filter.
```

Listing 5.13 displays the contents of gemini_css3_blur_filter.html that shows the code that Gemini generated in order to display a Web page that contains an artistic pattern of cubic Bezier curves with random radial gradients.

LISTING 5.13: gemini_css3_blur_filter.html

```
<!DOCTYPE html>
<html lang="en">
<head>
    <meta charset="UTF-8">
    <meta name="viewport" content="width=device-width,
                                initial-scale=1.0">
    <title>Blurred Box Shadow</title>
    <style>
        .blurred-box {
            width: 400px;
```

```
            height: 200px;
            background-color: lightblue;
            margin: 50px auto;
            box-shadow: inset 15px 12px 30px #000;
            filter: blur(5px);
        }
    </style>
</head>
<body>
    <div class="blurred-box"></div>
</body>
</html>
```

CSS Explanation

- `blurred-box:`
  - Sets the dimensions of our `div`.
  - `background-color` provides a base color to contrast with the shadow.
  - `margin` centers the box nicely.
  - `box-shadow: inset 15px 12px 30px #000`: Creates an inner shadow with the values as you specified.
  - `filter: blur(5px);`: Applies a 5-pixel blur to the entire element **including its shadow**.

Important things to note:

- **Inset Shadow:** Shadows rendered with the `inset` keyword fall *inside* the element.
- **Blur on Whole Element:** The CSS `filter: blur()` property blurs the entire element's contents and any shadows applied to it.

Customization:

- **Background:** Change the `background-color` to experiment with different visual effects.
- **Blur Intensity:** Modify the `blur()` value (e.g., `filter: blur(10px)`) to increase or decrease the blurriness.

Launch the Web page `gemini_css3_blur_filter.html` by navigating to the directory that contains this HTML Web page and then typing the following command:

```
open gemini_css3_blur_filter.html
```

After a few moments you will see the image in Figure 5.12 that displays a CSS3 blur filter effect.

FIGURE 5.12 CSS3 blur filter effect.

CSS3 DROP SHADOW

The following prompt was supplied to Gemini to generate an HTML Web page that contains an HTML <div> element that is rendered with a CSS3 drop-shadow effect.

```
Please generate an HTML Web page that contains a <div>
element of width 400 and height 200, with a box-shadow
attribute with value inset 15px 12px 30px #000.
```

Gemini:

Listing 5.14 displays the contents of gemini_css3_drop_shadow.html that shows the code that Gemini generated in order to display a Web page that contains a <div> element with a CSS3 blur filter and a box-shadow effect.

LISTING 5.14: gemini_css3_drop_shadow.html

```
<!DOCTYPE html>
<html>
<head>
  <title>Box Shadow Example</title>
  <style>
    .my-div {
      width: 400px;
      height: 200px;
      background-color: #f0f0f0;  /* A light background to
see the shadow */
      margin: 25px auto;          /* Center the div */
      box-shadow: inset 15px 12px 30px #000;
    }
```

```
    </style>
  </head>
<body>
  <div class="my-div"> </div>
</body>
</html>
```

Explanation:

CSS (<style> section):

.my-div: This is the CSS class applied to the <div>.
width: 400px; height: 200px;: Sets the dimensions of
                                              the box.
background-color: #f0f0f0;: Adds a light gray
            background to make the shadow more visible.
margin: 25px auto;: Centers the div horizontally on
                                            the page.
box-shadow: inset 15px 12px 30px #000;:
  inset: Creates an inner shadow.
  15px 12px: Horizontal and vertical offset of the
                                            shadow
  30px: Blur radius
  #000: Black color of the shadow

Launch the Web page gemini_css3_drop_shadow.html by navigating to the directory that contains this HTML Web page and then typing the following command:

```
open gemini_css3_drop_shadow.html
```

After a few moments you will see the image in Figure 5.13 that displays a CSS3 drop-shadow effect.

FIGURE 5.13 CSS3 drop-shadow effect.

SUMMARY

This chapter started with a brief description of the strengths and weaknesses of HTML, as well as popular use cases for HTML. Then you saw a Gemini-generated HTML Web page that contains a drop-down list with the days of the week.

Next, you learned about the strengths and weaknesses of CSS3, as well as use cases and potential security issues with CSS3. In addition, you saw code samples of CSS3 linear gradients, CSS3 radial gradients, rounded rectangles, diagonal gradients, and multigradients.

In addition, you learned how to create CSS3 animation effects, keyframe animation effects, and a carousel with CSS3. Furthermore, you learned how to use CSS3 2D transforms, quadratic Bezier curves, and cubic Bezier curves.

Finally, you saw examples of CSS3 filters, such as blur filters and drop-shadow filter effects.

6

INTRODUCTION TO SCALABLE VECTOR GRAPHICS (SVG)

This chapter gives you an overview of scalable vector graphics (SVG), along with various SVG code samples for rendering basic 2D shapes, linear gradients, radial gradients, and how to perform transformations. Note that the SVG code samples in this chapter were manually created, whereas the SVG code samples in Chapter 7 have been generated by Gemini.

The first section of this chapter shows you how to render polygons, ellipses, and circles in SVG. You will also learn how to create linear gradients and radial gradients that you can apply to 2D shapes. In addition, you will learn about quadratic Bezier curves and cubic Bezier curves, and also see examples of both in SVG.

The second section of this chapter introduces you to SVG filters, shadow effects, and text paths. You will also learn about SVG transforms and how to create SVG animation effects.

The third section of this chapter shows you how to combine SVG with JavaScript as well as CSS3. In addition, you will learn how to render bar charts using a combination of SVG and CSS3.

OVERVIEW OF SVG

This section contains various examples that illustrate some of the 2D shapes and effects that you can create with SVG. This section gives you a compressed overview, and if you want to learn more about SVG, you can perform an Internet search for details about books and many online tutorials.

SVG is an XML-based technology for rendering 2D shapes. SVG supports linear gradients, radial gradients, filter effects, transforms (translate, scale, skew, and rotate), and animation effects using an XML-based syntax. Although SVG does not support 3D effects, SVG provides functionality that is unavailable in CSS3, such as support for arbitrary polygons, elliptic arcs, quadratic and cubic Bezier curves, and filters.

Fortunately, you can reference SVG documents in CSS selectors via the CSS url() function, and the third part of this chapter contains examples of combining CSS3 and SVG in an HTML page. Moreover, the combination of CSS3 and SVG gives you a powerful mechanism for leveraging the functionality of SVG in CSS3 selectors. After reading this chapter you can learn more about SVG by performing an Internet search and then choosing from the many online tutorials that provide many SVG code samples.

Basic 2D Shapes in SVG

SVG supports a `<line>` element for rendering line segments, and its syntax looks like this:

```
<line x1="20" y1="20" x2="100" y2="150".../>
```

SVG `<line>` elements render line segments that connect the two points (x1,y1) and (x2,y2).

SVG also supports a `<rect>` element for rendering rectangles, and its syntax looks like this:

```
<rect width="200" height="50" x="20" y="50".../>
```

The SVG `<rect>` element renders a rectangle whose width and height are specified in the width and height attributes. The upper-left vertex of the rectangle is specified by the point with coordinates (x,y). Listing 6.1 displays the contents of `BasicShapes1.svg` that illustrates how to render line segments and rectangles.

LISTING 6.1 `BasicShapes1.svg`

```
<?xml version="1.0" encoding="iso-8859-1"?>
<!DOCTYPE svg PUBLIC "-//W3C//DTD SVG 20001102//EN"
"http://www.w3.org/TR/2000/CR-SVG-20001102/DTD/
                                    svg-20001102.dtd">

<svg xmlns="http://www.w3.org/2000/svg"
     xmlns:xlink="http://www.w3.org/1999/xlink"
     width="100%" height="100%">
<g>
<!-- left-side figures -->
<line x1="20" y1="20" x2="220" y2="20"
        stroke="blue" stroke-width="4"/>

<line x1="20" y1="40" x2="220" y2="40"
        stroke="red" stroke-width="10"/>
```

```
<rect width="200" height="50" x="20" y="70"
      fill="red" stroke="black" stroke-width="4"/>

<path d="M20,150 l200,0 l0,50 l-200,0 z"
      fill="blue" stroke="red" stroke-width="4"/>

<!-- right-side figures -->
<path d="M250,20 l200,0 l-100,50 z"
      fill="blue" stroke="red" stroke-width="4"/>

<path d="M300,100 l100,0 l50,50 l-50,50 l-100,0 l-50,-50 z"
      fill="yellow" stroke="red" stroke-width="4"/>
</g>
</svg>
```

The first SVG `<line>` element in Listing 6.1 specifies the color `blue` and a `stroke-width` (i.e., line width) of 4, whereas the second SVG `<line>` element specifies the color `red` and a `stroke-width` of 10.

Notice that the first SVG `<rect>` element renders a rectangle that looks the same (except for the color) as the second SVG `<line>` element, which shows you that you can use more than one SVG element to render a rectangle (or a line segment).

The SVG `<path>` element is probably the most flexible and powerful element, because you can create arbitrarily complex shapes, based on a concatenation of other SVG elements. Later in this chapter you will see an example of how to render multiple Bezier curves in an SVG `<path>` element.

An SVG `<path>` element contains a d attribute that specifies the points in the desired path. For example, the first SVG `<path>` element in Listing 6.1 contains the following d attribute:

```
d="M20,150 l200,0 l0,50 l-200,0 z"
```

This is how to interpret the contents of the d attribute:

- move to the absolute point (20,150)
- draw a horizontal line segment 200 pixels to the right
- draw a line segment 10 pixels to the right and 50 pixels down
- draw a horizontal line segment 200 pixels toward the left
- draw a line segment to the initial point (z)

Similar comments apply to the other two `<path>` elements in Listing 6.1. One thing to keep in mind is that uppercase letters (C, L, M, and Q) refer to absolute positions, whereas lowercase letters (c, l, m, and q) refer to relative positions with respect to the element that is to the immediate left. Experiment with the code in Listing 6.1 by using combinations of lowercase and uppercase letters to gain a better understanding of how to create different visual effects. Figure 6.1 displays the result of rendering the SVG document `BasicShapes1.svg`.

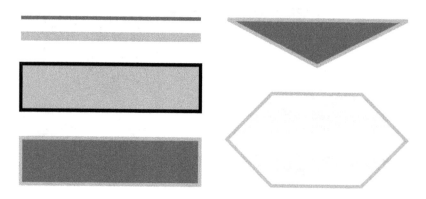

FIGURE 6.1 SVG line segments and rectangles.

SVG Gradients

As you have probably surmised, SVG supports linear gradients as well as radial gradients that you can apply to 2D shapes. For example, you can use the SVG `<path>` element to define elliptic arcs (using the `d` attribute) and then specify gradient effects. Note that SVG supports the `stroke-dasharray` attribute and the `<polygon>` element, neither of which is available in HTML5 `Canvas`. Listing 6.2 displays the contents of `BasicShapesLRG1.svg` that illustrates how to render 2D shapes with linear gradients and with radial gradients.

LISTING 6.2 `BasicShapesLRG1.svg`

```
<?xml version="1.0" encoding="iso-8859-1"?>
<!DOCTYPE svg PUBLIC "-//W3C//DTD SVG 20001102//EN"
  "http://www.w3.org/TR/2000/CR-SVG-20001102/DTD/
                                    svg-20001102.dtd">

<svg xmlns="http://www.w3.org/2000/svg"
     xmlns:xlink="http://www.w3.org/1999/xlink"
     width="100%" height="100%">
<defs>
<linearGradient id="pattern1"
                x1="0%" y1="100%" x2="100%" y2="0%">
<stop offset="0%"    stop-color="yellow"/>
<stop offset="40%"   stop-color="red"/>
<stop offset="80%"   stop-color="blue"/>
</linearGradient>

<radialGradient id="pattern2">
<stop offset="0%"    stop-color="yellow"/>
<stop offset="40%"   stop-color="red"/>
<stop offset="80%"   stop-color="blue"/>
</radialGradient>
```

```
</defs>

<g>
<ellipse cx="120" cy="80" rx="100" ry="50"
           fill="url(#pattern1)"/>

<ellipse cx="120" cy="200" rx="100" ry="50"
           fill="url(#pattern2)"/>

<ellipse cx="320" cy="80" rx="50" ry="50"
           fill="url(#pattern2)"/>

<path d="M 505,145 v -100 a 250,100 0 0,1 -200,100"
           fill="black"/>

<path d="M 500,140 v -100 a 250,100 0 0,1 -200,100"
           fill="url(#pattern1)"
           stroke="black" stroke-thickness="8"/>

<path d="M 305,165 v  100 a 250,100 0 0,1  200,-100"
           fill="black"/>

<path d="M 300,160 v  100 a 250,100 0 0,1  200,-100"
           fill="url(#pattern1)"
           stroke="black" stroke-thickness="8"/>

<ellipse cx="450" cy="240" rx="50" ry="50"
           fill="url(#pattern1)"/>
</g>
</svg>
```

Listing 6.2 contains an SVG <defs> element that specifies a <linearGradient> element (whose id attribute has value pattern1) with three stop values using an XML-based syntax, followed by a <radialGradient> element with three <stop> elements and an id attribute whose value is pattern2.

The SVG <g> element contains four <ellipse> elements, the first of which specifies the point (120, 80) as its center (cx, cy), with a major radius of 100, a minor radius of 50, filled with the linear gradient pattern1, as shown here:

```
<ellipse cx="120" cy="80" rx="100" ry="50"
           fill="url(#pattern1)"/>
```

Similar comments apply to the other three SVG <ellipse> elements.

The SVG <g> element also contains four <path> elements that render elliptic arcs. The first <path> element specifies a black background for the elliptic arc defined with the following d attribute:

```
d="M 505,145 v -100 a 250,100 0 0,1 -200,100"
```

Unfortunately, the SVG syntax for elliptic arcs is nonintuitive, and it's based on the notion of major arcs and minor arcs that connect two points on an ellipse. This example is only for illustrative purposes, so we won't delve into a detailed explanation of elliptic arcs work in SVG. If you need to learn the details, you can perform an Internet search and read the information found at the various links (be prepared to spend some time experimenting with how to generate various types of elliptic arcs).

The second SVG `<path>` element renders the same elliptic arc with a slight offset, using the linear gradient `pattern1`, which creates a shadow effect. Similar comments apply to the other pair of SVG `<path>` elements, which render an elliptic arc with the radial gradient `pattern2` (also with a shadow effect). Figure 6.2 displays the result of rendering `BasicShapesLRG1.svg`.

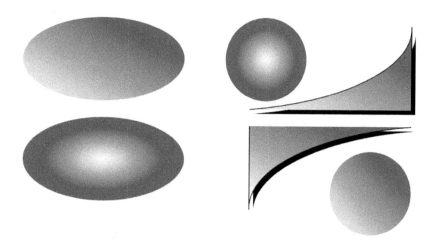

FIGURE 6.2 SVG elliptic arcs with linear and radial gradients.

SVG `<polygon>` Element

The SVG `<polygon>` element contains a polygon attribute in which you can specify points that represent the vertices of a polygon. The SVG `<polygon>` element is most useful when you want to create polygons with an arbitrary number of sides, but you can also use this element to render line segments and rectangles. Listing 6.3 displays the contents of `SvgCube1.svg` that illustrates how to render a cube in SVG.

LISTING 6.3 `SvgCube1.svg`

```
<?xml version="1.0" encoding="iso-8859-1"?>
<!DOCTYPE svg PUBLIC "-//W3C//DTD SVG 20001102//EN"
```

```
"http://www.w3.org/TR/2000/CR-SVG-20001102/DTD/
                              svg-20001102.dtd">

<svg xmlns="http://www.w3.org/2000/svg"
     xmlns:xlink="http://www.w3.org/1999/xlink"
     width="100%" height="100%">
<defs>
<linearGradient id="pattern1">
<stop offset="0%"    stop-color="yellow"/>
<stop offset="40%"   stop-color="red"/>
<stop offset="80%"   stop-color="blue"/>
</linearGradient>

<radialGradient id="pattern2">
<stop offset="0%"    stop-color="yellow"/>
<stop offset="40%"   stop-color="red"/>
<stop offset="80%"   stop-color="blue"/>
</radialGradient>

<radialGradient id="pattern3">
<stop offset="0%"    stop-color="red"/>
<stop offset="30%"   stop-color="yellow"/>
<stop offset="60%"   stop-color="white"/>
<stop offset="90%"   stop-color="blue"/>
</radialGradient>
</defs>

<!-- top face (counter clockwise) -->
<polygon fill="url(#pattern1)"
         points="50,50 200,50 240,30 90,30"/>

<!-- front face -->
<rect width="150" height="150" x="50" y="50"
         fill="url(#pattern2)"/>

<!-- right face (counter clockwise) -->
<polygon fill="url(#pattern3)"
         points="200,50 200,200 240,180 240,30"/>
</svg>
```

Listing 6.3 contains an SVG <defs> element that defines a linear gradient and two radial gradients. Next, the SVG <g> element contains the three faces of a cube: an SVG <polygon> element renders the top face (which is a parallelogram), an SVG <rect> element renders the front face, and another SVG <polygon> element renders the right face (also a parallelogram). The three faces of the cube are rendered with the linear gradient and the two radial gradients defined in the SVG <defs> element at the beginning of Listing 6.3. Figure 6.3 displays the result of rendering the SVG document SvgCube1.svg.

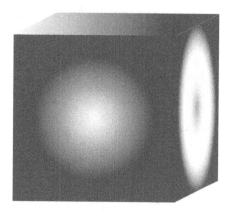

FIGURE 6.3 An SVG cube with gradient shading.

Bezier Curves

SVG supports quadratic and cubic Bezier curves that you can render with linear gradients or radial gradients. You can also concatenate multiple Bezier curves using an SVG <path> element. Listing 6.4 displays the contents of BezierCurves1.svg that illustrates how to render various Bezier curves.

LISTING 6.4 BezierCurves1.svg

```
<?xml version="1.0" encoding="iso-8859-1"?>
<!DOCTYPE svg PUBLIC "-//W3C//DTD SVG 20001102//EN"
  "http://www.w3.org/TR/2000/CR-SVG-20001102/DTD/
                                 svg-20001102.dtd">

<svg xmlns="http://www.w3.org/2000/svg"
     xmlns:xlink="http://www.w3.org/1999/xlink"
     width="100%" height="100%">
<defs>
<linearGradient id="pattern1"
                x1="0%" y1="100%" x2="100%" y2="0%">
<stop offset="0%"   stop-color="yellow"/>
<stop offset="40%"  stop-color="red"/>
<stop offset="80%"  stop-color="blue"/>
</linearGradient>

<linearGradient id="pattern2"
                gradientTransform="rotate(90)">
<stop offset="0%"   stop-color="#C0C040"/>
<stop offset="30%"  stop-color="#303000"/>
<stop offset="60%"  stop-color="#FF0F0F"/>
<stop offset="90%"  stop-color="#101000"/>
</linearGradient>
</defs>
```

```
<g transform="scale(1.5,0.5)">
<path d="m 0,50 C 400,200 200,-150 100,350"
        stroke="black" stroke-width="4"
        fill="url(#pattern1)"/>
</g>

<g transform="translate(50,50)">
<g transform="scale(0.5,1)">
<path d="m 50,50 C 400,100 200,200 100,20"
        fill="red" stroke="black" stroke-width="4"/>
</g>

<g transform="scale(1,1)">
<path d="m 50,50 C 400,100 200,200 100,20"
        fill="yellow" stroke="black" stroke-width="4"/>
</g>
</g>

<g transform="translate(-50,50)">
<g transform="scale(1,2)">
<path d="M 50,50 C 400,100 200,200 100,20"
        fill="blue" stroke="black" stroke-width="4"/>
</g>
</g>

<g transform="translate(-50,50)">
<g transform="scale(0.5, 0.5) translate(195,345)">
<path d="m20,20 C20,50 20,450 300,200 s-150,-250 200,100"
        fill="blue" style="stroke:#880088;stroke-
width:4;"/>
</g>

<g transform="scale(0.5, 0.5) translate(185,335)">
<path d="m20,20 C20,50 20,450 300,200 s-150,-250 200,100"
        fill="url(#pattern2)"
style="stroke:#880088;stroke-width:4;"/>
</g>

<g transform="scale(0.5, 0.5) translate(180,330)">
<path d="m20,20 C20,50 20,450 300,200 s-150,-250 200,100"
      fill="blue" style="stroke:#880088;stroke-width:4;"/>
</g>

<g transform="scale(0.5, 0.5) translate(170,320)">
<path d="m20,20 C20,50 20,450 300,200 s-150,-250 200,100"
        fill="url(#pattern2)" style="stroke:black;stroke-
                                            width:4;"/>
</g>
</g>

<g transform="scale(0.8,1) translate(380,120)">
```

```
<path d="M0,0 C200,150 400,300 20,250"
      fill="url(#pattern2)" style="stroke:blue;stroke-
                                           width:4;"/>
</g>

<g transform="scale(2.0,2.5) translate(150,-80)">
<path d="M200,150 C0,0 400,300 20,250"
      fill="url(#pattern2)" style="stroke:blue;stroke-
                                           width:4;"/>
</g>
</svg>
```

Listing 6.4 contains an SVG <defs> element that defines two linear gradients, followed by 10 SVG <path> elements, each of which renders a cubic Bezier curve. The SVG <path> elements are enclosed in SVG <g> elements whose transform attributes contain the SVG scale() function or the SVGtranslate() functions (or both).

The first SVG <g> element invokes the SVG scale() function to scale the cubic Bezier curve that is specified in an SVG <path> element, as shown here:

```
<g transform="scale(1.5,0.5)">
<path d="m 0,50 C 400,200 200,-150 100,350"
      stroke="black" stroke-width="4"
      fill="url(#pattern1)"/>
</g>
```

The cubic Bezier curve has an initial point (0,50), with control points (400,200) and (200,-150), followed by the second control point (100,350). The Bezier curve is black, with a width of 4, and its fill color is defined in the <linearGradient> element (whose id attribute is pattern1) that is contained in the SVG <defs> element. The remaining SVG <path> elements are similar to the first SVG <path> element, so they will not be described. Figure 6.4 displays the result of rendering the Bezier curves that are defined in the SVG document BezierCurves1.svg.

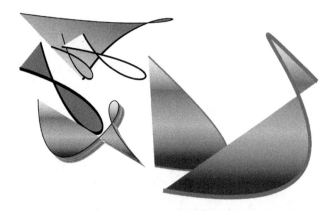

FIGURE 6.4 SVG Bezier curves.

SVG FILTERS, SHADOW EFFECTS, AND TEXT PATHS

You can create filter effects that you can apply to 2D shapes and also to text strings; this section contains three SVG-based examples of creating such effects. Listing 6.5, Listing 6.6, and Listing 6.7 display the contents of the SVG documents `BlurFilterText1.svg`, `ShadowFilterText1.svg`, and `TextOnQBezierPath1.svg`, respectively.

LISTING 6.5 `BlurFilterText1.svg`

```
<?xml version="1.0" encoding="iso-8859-1"?>
<!DOCTYPE svg PUBLIC "-//W3C//DTD SVG 20001102//EN"
  "http://www.w3.org/TR/2000/CR-SVG-20001102/DTD/
                               svg-20001102.dtd">

<svg xmlns="http://www.w3.org/2000/svg"
     xmlns:xlink="http://www.w3.org/1999/xlink"
     width="100%" height="100%">
<defs>
<filter
     id="blurFilter1"
     filterUnits="objectBoundingBox"
     x="0" y="0"
     width="100%" height="100%">
<feGaussianBlur stdDeviation="4"/>
</filter>
</defs>

<g transform="translate(50,100)">
<text id="normalText" x="0" y="0"
      fill="red" stroke="black" stroke-width="4"
      font-size="72">
    Normal Text
</text>

<text id="horizontalText" x="0" y="100"
      filter="url(#blurFilter1)"
      fill="red" stroke="black" stroke-width="4"
      font-size="72">
    Blurred Text
</text>
</g>
</svg>
```

The SVG `<defs>` element in Listing 6.5 contains an SVG `<filter>` element that specifies a Gaussian blur with the following line:

```
<feGaussianBlur stdDeviation="4"/>
```

You can specify larger values for the `stdDeviation` attribute if you want to create more diffuse filter effects.

The first SVG <text> element that is contained in the SVG <g> element renders a normal text string, whereas the second SVG <text> element contains a filter attribute that references the filter (defined in the SVG <defs> element) in order to render the same text string, as shown here:

```
filter="url(#blurFilter1)"
```

Figure 6.5 displays the result of rendering BlurFilterText1.svg that creates a filter effect.

FIGURE 6.5 SVG filter effect.

LISTING 6.6 ShadowFilterText1.svg

```
<?xml version="1.0" encoding="iso-8859-1"?>
<!DOCTYPE svg PUBLIC "-//W3C//DTD SVG 20001102//EN"
 "http://www.w3.org/TR/2000/CR-SVG-20001102/DTD/
                                    svg-20001102.dtd">

<svg xmlns="http://www.w3.org/2000/svg"
     xmlns:xlink="http://www.w3.org/1999/xlink"
     width="100%" height="100%">
<defs>
<filter
     id="blurFilter1"
     filterUnits="objectBoundingBox"
     x="0" y="0"
     width="100%" height="100%">
<feGaussianBlur stdDeviation="4"/>
</filter>
</defs>

<g transform="translate(50,150)">
<text id="horizontalText" x="15" y="15"
      filter="url(#blurFilter1)"
      fill="red" stroke="black" stroke-width="2"
      font-size="72">
     Shadow Text
</text>
```

```
<text id="horizontalText" x="0" y="0"
      fill="red" stroke="black" stroke-width="4"
      font-size="72">
   Shadow Text
</text>
</g>
</svg>
```

Listing 6.6 contains two SVG `<text>` elements that specify the value 2 and the value 4, respectively, for the `stroke-width` attribute, thereby creating a shadow effect.

Figure 6.6 displays the result of rendering `ShadowFilterText1.svg` that creates a shadow effect.

FIGURE 6.6 SVG text with a shadow effect.

LISTING 6.7 `TextOnQBezierPath1.svg`

```
<?xml version="1.0" encoding="iso-8859-1"?>
<!DOCTYPE svg PUBLIC "-//W3C//DTD SVG 20001102//EN"
  "http://www.w3.org/TR/2000/CR-SVG-20001102/DTD/
                              svg-20001102.dtd">

<svg xmlns="http://www.w3.org/2000/svg"
     xmlns:xlink="http://www.w3.org/1999/xlink"
     width="100%" height="100%">
<defs>
<path id="pathDefinition"
      d="m0,0 Q100,0 200,200 T300,200 z"/>
</defs>

<g transform="translate(100,100)">
<text id="textStyle" fill="red"
      stroke="blue" stroke-width="2"
      font-size="24">

<textPath xlink:href="#pathDefinition">
      Sample Text that follows a path specified by a
quadratic Bezier curve
</textPath>
</text>
</g>
</svg>
```

The SVG `<defs>` element in Listing 6.7 contains an SVG `<path>` element that defines a quadratic Bezier curve (note the Q in the d attribute). This SVG `<path>` element has an `id` attribute whose value is `pathDefinition` and is referenced later in this code sample.

The SVG `<g>` element contains an SVG `<text>` element that specifies a text string to render, as well as an SVG `<textPath>` element that specifies the path along which the text is rendered, as shown here:

```
<textPath xlink:href="#pathDefinition">
        Sample Text that follows a path specified by a
Quadratic Bezier curve
</textPath>
```

Notice that the SVG `<textPath>` element contains the attribute `xlink:href` whose value is `pathDefinition`, which is also the `id` of the SVG `<path>` element that is defined in the SVG `<defs>` element. As a result, the text string is rendered along the path of a quadratic Bezier curve instead of rendering the text string horizontally (which is the default behavior). Figure 6.7 displays the result of rendering `TextOnQBezierPath1.svg`, that renders a text string along the path of a quadratic Bezier curve.

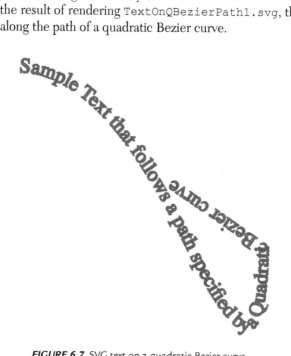

FIGURE 6.7 SVG text on a quadratic Bezier curve.

SVG TRANSFORMS

Earlier in this chapter you saw some examples of SVG transform effects. In addition to the SVG functions `scale()`, `translate()`, and `rotate()`, SVG provides the `skew()` function to create skew effects. Listing 6.8 displays the contents of `TransformEffects1.svg` that illustrates how to apply transforms to rectangles and circles in SVG.

LISTING 6.8 `TransformEffects1.svg`

```
<?xml version="1.0" encoding="iso-8859-1"?>
<!DOCTYPE svg PUBLIC "-//W3C//DTD SVG 20001102//EN"
 "http://www.w3.org/TR/2000/CR-SVG-20001102/DTD/
                                svg-20001102.dtd">


<svg xmlns="http://www.w3.org/2000/svg"
    xmlns:xlink="http://www.w3.org/1999/xlink"
    width="100%" height="100%">
<defs>
<linearGradient id="gradientDefinition1"
    x1="0" y1="0" x2="200" y2="0"
    gradientUnits="userSpaceOnUse">
<stop offset="0%"   style="stop-color:#FF0000"/>
<stop offset="100%" style="stop-color:#440000"/>
</linearGradient>

<pattern id="dotPattern" width="8" height="8"
         patternUnits="userSpaceOnUse">

<circle id="circle1" cx="2" cy="2" r="2"
        style="fill:red;"/>
</pattern>
</defs>

<!-- full cylinder -->
<g id="largeCylinder" transform="translate(100,20)">
<ellipse cx="0"  cy="50" rx="20" ry="50"
            stroke="blue" stroke-width="4"
            style="fill:url(#gradientDefinition1)"/>

<rect x="0" y="0" width="300" height="100"
        style="fill:url(#gradientDefinition1)"/>

<rect x="0" y="0" width="300" height="100"
        style="fill:url(#dotPattern)"/>

<ellipse cx="300" cy="50" rx="20"  ry="50"
            stroke="blue" stroke-width="4"
            style="fill:yellow;"/>
</g>

<!-- half-sized cylinder -->
<g transform="translate(100,100) scale(.5)">
<use xlink:href="#largeCylinder" x="0" y="0"/>
</g>
```

```
<!-- skewed cylinder -->
<g transform="translate(100,100) skewX(40) skewY(20)">
<use xlink:href="#largeCylinder" x="0" y="0"/>
</g>

<!-- rotated cylinder -->
<g transform="translate(100,100) rotate(40)">
<use xlink:href="#largeCylinder" x="0" y="0"/>
</g>
</svg>
```

The SVG `<defs>` element in Listing 6.8 contains a `<linearGradient>` element that defines a linear gradient, followed by an SVG `<pattern>` element that defines a custom pattern as shown here:

```
<pattern id="dotPattern" width="8" height="8"
         patternUnits="userSpaceOnUse">

<circle id="circle1" cx="2" cy="2" r="2"
        style="fill:red;"/>
</pattern>
```

As you can see, the SVG `<pattern>` element contains an SVG `<circle>` element that is repeated in a grid-like fashion inside an 8x8 rectangle (note the values of the width attribute and the height attribute). The SVG `<pattern>` element has an `id` attribute whose value is `dotPattern` because, as you will see, this element creates a "dotted" effect.

Listing 6.8 contains four SVG `<g>` elements, each of which renders a cylinder that references the SVG `<pattern>` element that is defined in the SVG `<defs>` element. The first SVG `<g>` element in Listing 6.8 contains two `<ellipse>` elements and two SVG `<rect>` elements. The first `<ellipse>` element renders the left-side "cover" of the cylinder with the linear gradient that is defined in the SVG `<defs>` element. The first `<rect>` element renders the "body" of the cylinder with a linear gradient, and the second `<rect>` element renders the "dot pattern" on the body of the cylinder. Finally, the second `<ellipse>` element renders the right-side "cover" of the ellipse.

The other three cylinders are easy to create: they simply reference the first cylinder and apply a transformation to change the size, shape, and orientation. Specifically, these three cylinders reference the first cylinder with the following code:

```
<use xlink:href="#largeCylinder" x="0" y="0"/>
```

and then they apply scale, skew, and rotate functions in order to render scaled, skewed, and rotated cylinders. Figure 6.8 displays the result of rendering `TransformEffects1.svg`.

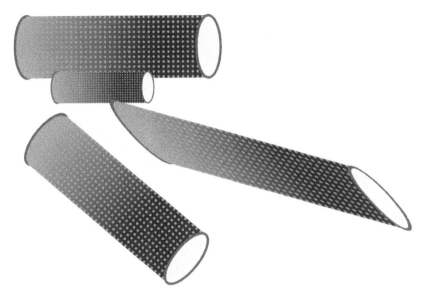

FIGURE 6.8 SVG transform effects.

SVG ANIMATION

SVG supports animation effects that you can specify as part of the declaration of SVG elements. Listing 6.9displays the contents of the SVG document AnimateMultiRect1.svg, which illustrates how to create an animation effect with four rectangles.

LISTING 6.9 `AnimateMultiRect1.svg`

```
<?xml version="1.0" encoding="iso-8859-1"?>
<!DOCTYPE svg PUBLIC "-//W3C//DTD SVG 20010904//EN"
  "http://www.w3.org/TR/2001/REC-SVG-20010904/DTD/
                                         svg10.dtd">

<svg xmlns="http://www.w3.org/2000/svg"
    xmlns:xlink="http://www.w3.org/1999/xlink"
    width="100%" height="100%">
<defs>
<rect id="rect1" width="100" height="100"
      stroke-width="1" stroke="blue"/>
</defs>

<g transform="translate(10,10)">
<rect width="500" height="400"
      fill="none" stroke-width="4" stroke="black"/>
</g>
```

```
<g transform="translate(10,10)">
<use xlink:href="#rect1" x="0" y="0" fill="red">
<animate attributeName="x" attributeType="XML"
                begin="0s" dur="4s"
                fill="freeze" from="0" to="400"/>
</use>

<use xlink:href="#rect1" x="400" y="0" fill="green">
<animate attributeName="y" attributeType="XML"
                begin="0s" dur="4s"
                fill="freeze" from="0" to="300"/>
</use>

<use xlink:href="#rect1" x="400" y="300" fill="blue">
<animate attributeName="x" attributeType="XML"
                begin="0s" dur="4s"
                fill="freeze" from="400" to="0"/>
</use>

<use xlink:href="#rect1" x="0" y="300" fill="yellow">
<animate attributeName="y" attributeType="XML"
                begin="0s" dur="4s"
                fill="freeze" from="300" to="0"/>
</use>
</g>
</svg>
```

The SVG <defs> element in Listing 6.9 contains an SVG <rect> element that defines a blue rectangle, followed by an SVG <g> element that renders the border of a large rectangle that "contains" the animation effect, which involves the movement of four rectangles in a clockwise fashion along the perimeter of an outer rectangle.

The second SVG <g> element contains four <use> elements that perform a parallel animation effect on four rectangles. The first <use> element references the rectangle defined in the SVG <defs> element and then animates the x attribute during a four-second interval as shown here:

```
<use xlink:href="#rect1" x="0" y="0" fill="red">
<animate attributeName="x" attributeType="XML"
                begin="0s" dur="4s"
                fill="freeze" from="0" to="400"/>
</use>
```

Notice that the x attribute varies from 0 to 400, which moves the rectangle horizontally from left to right. The second SVG <use> element also references the rectangle defined in the SVG <defs> element, except that the animation involves changing the y attribute from 0 to 300 in order to move the rectangle downward, as shown here:

```
<use xlink:href="#rect1" x="400" y="0" fill="green">
<animate attributeName="y" attributeType="XML"
```

```
                  begin="0s" dur="4s"
                  fill="freeze" from="0" to="300"/>
</use>
```

In a similar fashion, the third SVG <use> element moves the referenced rectangle horizontally from right to left, and the fourth SVG <use> element moves the referenced rectangle vertically and upward.

If you want to create a sequential animation effect (or a combination of sequential and parallel), then you need to modify the values of the begin attribute (and possibly the dur attribute) in order to achieve your desired animation effect. Figure 6.9 displays the result of rendering AnimateMultiRect1.svg.

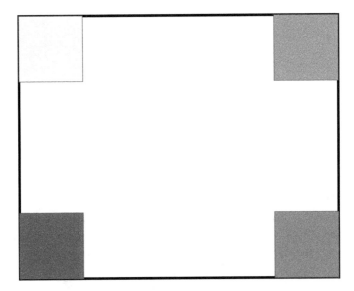

FIGURE 6.9 SVG animation effect with four rectangles.

Listing 6.10 displays the contents of the SVG document AnimateText1.svg that illustrates how to animate a text string.

LISTING 6.10 AnimateText1.svg

```
<?xml version="1.0" encoding="iso-8859-1"?>
<!DOCTYPE svg PUBLIC "-//W3C//DTD SVG 20010904//EN"
  "http://www.w3.org/TR/2001/REC-SVG-20010904/DTD/
                                              svg10.dtd">

<svg xmlns="http://www.w3.org/2000/svg"
     xmlns:xlink="http://www.w3.org/1999/xlink"
     width="100%" height="100%">

<g transform="translate(100,100)">
<text x="0" y="0" font-size="48" visibility="hidden"
```

```
          stroke="black" stroke-width="2">
       Animating Text in SVG
<set attributeName="visibility"
          attributeType="CSS" to="visible"
          begin="2s" dur="5s" fill="freeze"/>

<animateMotion path="M0,0 L50,150"
          begin="2s" dur="5s" fill="freeze"/>

<animateColor attributeName="fill"
          attributeType="CSS"
          from="yellow" to="red"
          begin="2s" dur="8s" fill="freeze"/>

<animateTransform attributeName="transform"
          attributeType="XML"
          type="rotate" from="-90" to="0"
          begin="2s" dur="5s" fill="freeze"/>

<animateTransform attributeName="transform"
          attributeType="XML"
          type="scale" from=".5" to="1.5" additive="sum"
          begin="2s" dur="5s" fill="freeze"/>
</text>
</g>
</svg>
```

Listing 6.10 contains an SVG <text> element that specifies four different effects. The <set> element specifies the visibility of the text string for a five-second interval with an initial offset of two seconds.

The SVG <animateMotion> element shifts the upper-left corner of the text string from the point (0,0) to the point (50,150) in a linear fashion. This effect is combined with two other motion effects: rotation and scaling.

The SVG <animateColor> element changes the text color from yellow to red, and because the dur attribute has value 8s, this effect lasts three seconds longer than the other animation effects, whose dur attributes have values 5s. Note that all the animation effects start at the same time.

The first SVG <animateTransform> element performs a clockwise rotation of 90 degrees from vertical to horizontal. The second SVG <animateTransform> element performs a scaling effect that occurs in parallel with the first SVG <animateTransform> element because they have the same values for the begin attribute and the dur attribute. Figure 6.10 displays the result of rendering AnimateText1.svg.

Animating Text in SVG

FIGURE 6.10 SVG text animation effect.

SVG AND JAVASCRIPT

SVG allows you to embed JavaScript in a CDATA section, which means that you can programmatically create SVG elements. Listing 6.11 displays the contents of the SVG document `ArchEllipses1.svg` that illustrates how to render a set of ellipses that follow the path of an Archimedean spiral.

LISTING 6.11 `ArchEllipses1.svg`

```
<?xml version="1.0" standalone="no"?>
<!DOCTYPE svg PUBLIC "-//W3C//DTD SVG 20010904//EN"
  "http://www.w3.org/TR/2001/REC-SVG-20010904/DTD/
                                          svg10.dtd">


<svg xmlns="http://www.w3.org/2000/svg"
     xmlns:xlink="http://www.w3.org/1999/xlink"
     onload="init(evt)"
     width="100%" height="100%">

<script type="text/ecmascript">
<![CDATA[
    var basePointX   = 250;
    var basePointY   = 200;
    var currentX     = 0;
    var currentY     = 0;
    var offsetX      = 0;
    var offsetY      = 0;
    var radius       = 0;
    var minorAxis    = 60;
    var majorAxis    = 30;
    var spiralCount  = 4;
    var Constant     = 0.25;
    var angle        = 0;
    var maxAngle     = 720;
    var angleDelta   = 2;
    var strokeWidth  = 1;
    var redColor     = "rgb(255,0,0)";

    var ellipseNode  = null;
    var svgDocument  = null;
    var target       = null;
    var gcNode       = null;

    var svgNS        = "http://www.w3.org/2000/svg";

    function init(event)
    {
        svgDocument = event.target.ownerDocument;
        gcNode = svgDocument.getElementById("gc");
```

```
        drawSpiral(event);
    }


    function drawSpiral(event)
    {
        for(angle=0; angle<maxAngle; angle+=angleDelta)
        {
            radius   = Constant*angle;
            offsetX  = radius*Math.cos(angle*Math.PI/180);
            offsetY  = radius*Math.sin(angle*Math.PI/180);
            currentX = basePointX+offsetX;
            currentY = basePointY-offsetY;

            ellipseNode =
                    svgDocument.createElementNS(svgNS,
                                            "ellipse");

            ellipseNode.setAttribute("fill", redColor);
            ellipseNode.setAttribute("stroke-width",
                                            strokeWidth);

            if( angle % 3 == 0 ) {
                ellipseNode.setAttribute("stroke", "yellow");
            } else {
                ellipseNode.setAttribute("stroke", "green");
            }

            ellipseNode.setAttribute("cx", currentX);
            ellipseNode.setAttribute("cy", currentY);
            ellipseNode.setAttribute("rx", majorAxis);
            ellipseNode.setAttribute("ry", minorAxis);

            gcNode.appendChild(ellipseNode);
        }
    } // drawSpiral
  ]]></script>
<!-- =============================== -->
<g id="gc" transform="translate(10,10)">
<rect x="0" y="0"
            width="800" height="500"
            fill="none" stroke="none"/>
</g>
</svg>
```

Notice that the SVG <svg> element in Listing 6.11 contains an onload attribute that references the JavaScript function init(), and as you can surmise, the init() function is executed when you launch this SVG document in a browser. In this example, the purpose of the init() function is to reference the graphics context that is defined in the SVG <g> element at the bottom of Listing 6.11, and then to invoke the drawSpiral() function.

Whenever you want to include JavaScript in an SVG document, you need to place the JavaScript code inside a CDATA section that is embedded in a `<script>` element. The CDATA section in Listing 6.11 initializes some variables, along with the definition of the `init()` function and the `drawSpiral()` function.

The code in the `drawSpiral()` function consists of a loop that renders a set of dynamically created SVG `<ellipse>` elements. Each SVG `<ellipse>` element is created in the SVG namespace that is specified in the variable `svgNS`, after which values are assigned to the required attributes of an ellipse, as shown here:

```
ellipseNode = svgDocument.createElementNS(svgNS, "ellipse");
ellipseNode.setAttribute("fill", redColor);
ellipseNode.setAttribute("stroke-width", strokeWidth);

// conditional logic omitted
ellipseNode.setAttribute("cx", currentX);
ellipseNode.setAttribute("cy", currentY);
ellipseNode.setAttribute("rx", majorAxis);
ellipseNode.setAttribute("ry", minorAxis);
```

After each SVG `<ellipse>` element is dynamically created, the element is appended to the DOM with one line of code, as shown here:

```
gcNode.appendChild(ellipseNode);
```

Finally, the SVG `<g>` element at the bottom of Listing 6.11 acts as a canvas on which the dynamically generated ellipses are rendered. Figure 6.11 displays the result of rendering `ArchEllipses1.svg`.

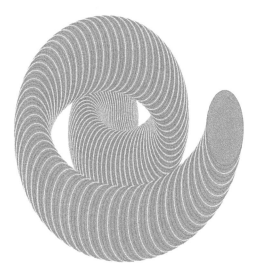

FIGURE 6.11 Dynamically generated SVG `<ellipse>`elements.

CSS3 AND SVG BAR CHARTS

Now that you know how to reference SVG documents in CSS3 selectors, let's look at an example of referencing an SVG-based bar chart in a CSS3 selector. Listing 6.12 displays the contents of the HTML5 page CSS3SVGBarChart1.html, Listing 6.13 displays the contents of the CSS3 style sheet CSS3SVGBarChart1.css (whose selectors are applied to the contents of Listing 6.13), and Listing 6.14 displays the contents of the SVG document CSS3SVGBarChart1.svg (referenced in a selector in Listing 6.13) that contains the SVG code for rendering a bar chart.

LISTING 6.12 CSS3SVGBarChart1.html

```
<!doctype html>
<html en>
<head>
<title>CSS Multi Column Text and SVG Bar Chart</title>
<meta charset="utf-8" />
<link href="CSS3SVGBarChart1.css" rel="stylesheet"
                                   type="text/css">
</head>

<body>
<div id="outer">
<article>
<p id="line1">.</p>
<div id="columns">
<p>
CSS enables you to define so-called "selectors" that specify
the style or the manner in which you want to render
elements in an HTML page.  CSS helps you modularize your
HTML content and since you can place your CSS definitions in
a separate file, you can also reuse the same CSS definitions
in multiple HTML files.</p>
<p>
Moreover, CSS also enables you to simplify the updates that
you need to make to elements in HTML pages. For example,
suppose that multiple HTML table elements use a CSS rule
that specifies the color red. If you later need to change
the color to blue, you can effect such a change simply by
making one change (i.e., changing red to blue) in one CSS
rule.</p>
<p>
Without a CSS rule, you would be forced to manually update
the color attribute in every HTML table element that
is affected, which is error-prone, time-consuming, and
extremely inefficient.</p>
<p>
 As you can see, it's very easy to reference an SVG
document in CSS selectors, and in this example, an
```

```
SVG-based bar chart is rendered on the left side of the
screen.</p>
</div>

<p id="line1">.</p>
</article>
</div>
<div id="chart1">
</div>
</body>
</html>
```

In Chapter 4, you saw an example of rendering multicolumn text, and the contents of Listing 6.12 are essentially the same as the contents of that example. There is an additional HTML <div> element (whose id attribute has value chart1), however, that is used for rendering an SVG bar chart via a CSS selector in Listing 6.13.

LISTING 6.13 CSS3SVGBarChart1.css

```
#columns {
-webkit-column-count : 4;
-webkit-column-gap : 40px;
-webkit-column-rule : 1px solid rgb(255,255,255);
column-count : 3;
column-gap : 40px;
column-rule : 1px solid rgb(255,255,255);
}

#line1 {
color: red;
font-size: 24px;
background-image: -webkit-gradient(linear, 0% 0%, 0% 100%,
                            from(#fff), to(#f00));
background-image: -gradient(linear, 0% 0%, 0% 100%,
                            from(#fff), to(#f00));
-webkit-border-radius: 4px;
border-radius: 4px;
}

#chart1 {
opacity: 0.5;
color: red;
width: 800px;
height: 50%;
position: absolute; top: 20px; left: 20px;
font-size: 24px;
-webkit-border-radius: 4px;
-moz-border-radius: 4px;
border-radius: 4px;
border-radius: 4px;
```

```
-webkit-background: url(CSS3SVGBarChart1.svg) top right;
-moz-background: url(CSS3SVGBarChart1.svg) top right;
background: url(CSS3SVGBarChart1.svg) top right;
}
```

The #chart selector contains various attributes, along with a reference to an SVG document that renders an actual bar chart, as shown here:

```
-webkit-background: url(CSS3SVGBarChart1.svg) top right;
-moz-background: url(CSS3SVGBarChart1.svg) top right;
background: url(CSS3SVGBarChart1.svg) top right;
```

Now that you've seen the contents of the HTML5 page and the selectors in the CSS style sheet, let's take a look at the SVG document that renders the bar chart.

LISTING 6.14 CSS3SVGBarChart1.svg

```
<?xml version="1.0" encoding="iso-8859-1"?>
<!DOCTYPE svg PUBLIC "-//W3C//DTD SVG 20001102//EN"
 "http://www.w3.org/TR/2000/CR-SVG-20001102/DTD/
                                    svg-20001102.dtd">

<svg xmlns="http://www.w3.org/2000/svg"
     xmlns:xlink="http://www.w3.org/1999/xlink"
     width="100%" height="100%">
<defs>
<linearGradient id="pattern1">
<stop offset="0%"  stop-color="yellow"/>
<stop offset="40%"  stop-color="red"/>
<stop offset="80%"  stop-color="blue"/>
</linearGradient>

<radialGradient id="pattern2">
<stop offset="0%"  stop-color="yellow"/>
<stop offset="40%"  stop-color="red"/>
<stop offset="80%"  stop-color="blue"/>
</radialGradient>

<radialGradient id="pattern3">
<stop offset="0%"  stop-color="red"/>
<stop offset="30%"  stop-color="yellow"/>
<stop offset="60%"  stop-color="white"/>
<stop offset="90%"  stop-color="blue"/>
</radialGradient>
</defs>

<g id="chart1" transform="translate(0,0) scale(1,1)">
<rect width="30" height="235" x="15"  y="15"  fill="black"/>
<rect width="30" height="240" x="10"  y="10"
                                    fill="url(#pattern1)"/>
```

```
<rect width="30" height="145" x="45"  y="105" fill="black"/>
<rect width="30" height="150" x="40"  y="100"
                             fill="url(#pattern2)"/>


<rect width="30" height="195" x="75"  y="55"  fill="black"/>
<rect width="30" height="200" x="70"  y="50"
                             fill="url(#pattern1)"/>


<rect width="30" height="185" x="105" y="65"  fill="black"/>
<rect width="30" height="190" x="100" y="60"
                             fill="url(#pattern3)"/>


<rect width="30" height="145" x="135" y="105" fill="black"/>
<rect width="30" height="150" x="130" y="100"
 fill="url(#pattern1)"/>


<rect width="30" height="225" x="165" y="25"  fill="black"/>
<rect width="30" height="230" x="160" y="20"
                             fill="url(#pattern2)"/>


<rect width="30" height="145" x="195" y="105" fill="black"/>
<rect width="30" height="150" x="190" y="100"
                             fill="url(#pattern1)"/>


<rect width="30" height="175" x="225" y="75"  fill="black"/>
<rect width="30" height="180" x="220" y="70"
                             fill="url(#pattern3)"/>
</g>

<g id="chart2" transform="translate(250,125) scale(1,0.5)"
                             width="100%" height="100%">
<use xlink:href="#chart1"/>
</g>
</svg>
```

Listing 6.14 contains an SVG <defs> element in which three gradients are defined (one linear gradient and two radial gradients), whose id attribute has values pattern1, pattern2, and pattern3, respectively. These gradients are referenced by their id in the SVG <g> element that renders a set of rectangular bars for a bar chart. The second SVG <g> element (whose id attribute has value chart2) performs a transform involving the SVG translate() and scale() functions, and then renders the actual bar chart, as shown in this code:

```
<g id="chart2" transform="translate(250,125) scale(1,0.5)"
                             width="100%" height="100%">
<use xlink:href="#chart1"/>
</g>
```

Figure 6.12 displays the result of applying CSS3SVGBarChart1.css to the elements in the HTML page CSS3SVGBarChart1.html.

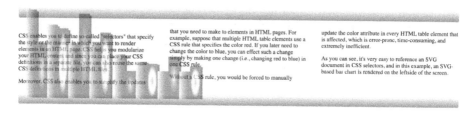

FIGURE 6.12 CSS3 with SVG applied to an HTML page.

SUMMARY

This chapter gave you an introduction to SVG, and you saw several code samples that illustrated the graphics capabilities of SVG. You also learned how to render 2D shapes and how to combine the functionality of SVG with CSS3. In particular, you learned how to do the following:

- create SVG linear gradients and radial gradients
- apply SVG gradients to ellipses and elliptic arcs
- render quadratic Bezier curves and cubic Bezier curves in SVG
- reference SVG documents in CSS3 selectors

You also learned how to combine SVG with JavaScript and how to create bar charts using a combination of SVG and CSS3.

7

SCALABLE VECTOR GRAPHICS (SVG) AND GEMINI

This chapter provides an assortment of scalable vector graphics (SVG)-based code samples that are generated by Gemini, based on prompts that are supplied to Gemini. Some of the code samples will be familiar: the difference is that almost all the code samples in this chapter are generated by Gemini.

The first section of this chapter describes the strengths and weaknesses of SVG, followed by SVG use cases, SVG accessibility, and potential security issues with SVG.

The second portion of this chapter contains examples of Gemini generating linear gradients, radial gradients, and various SVG 2D shapes and gradients. You will also see how to render a bar chart in SVG.

The third section shows you how to render quadratic Bezier curves and cubic Bezier curves, as well as how to add animation effects for Bezier curves. In addition, you will learn how to create hover effects.

The fourth section compares SVG with CSS3 and also compares SVG with PNGs. Then you will learn how to work with SVG filters, such as blur filters and turbulence filters.

The fifth section contains code samples that combine SVG and CSS3 in an HTML Web page, as well as combining SVG and JavaScript in an HTML Web page. You will learn how to create other effects that involve JavaScript and SVG, such as rendering checkerboard patterns.

One more detail to keep in mind: the SVG code samples involving Bezier curves (toward the end of the chapter) are created by Python code that is generated by Gemini. Many laptops have Python already installed, and if need be, you can search online with the keywords "install Python Windows" to find links where you can download Python onto your laptop (and also replace "Windows" with your operating system).

WORKING WITH SVG

The following prompt was supplied to Gemini to describe SVG and its various features.

```
Please provide a description of the features of SVG, along
with its strengths and weaknesses.
```

```
Gemini:
```

SVG is a versatile image format used on the Web and in various applications. Here is a description of its features, along with its strengths and weaknesses:

Features of SVG

1. **Vector-Based**: Unlike raster images like JPEGs or PNGs, SVGs are composed of vectors, which are mathematical descriptions of the image's shapes and paths. This allows them to scale infinitely without losing quality.

2. **XML-Based**: SVG images are written in XML (Extensible Markup Language), making them easily readable and modifiable by both humans and machines.

3. **Interactive and Dynamic**: SVGs can be manipulated using CSS and JavaScript, allowing for interactivity, animation, and dynamic changes.

4. **DOM Integration**: SVG elements are part of the Document Object Model (DOM), meaning they can be interacted with just like HTML elements, offering a wide range of manipulation possibilities.

5. **Styling and Animation**: SVG supports styling with CSS and can be animated using CSS animations or SMIL (Synchronized Multimedia Integration Language).

6. **Accessibility**: Texts in SVG images are selectable and searchable, improving accessibility and SEO.

7. **Compact File Size**: Generally, SVG files are smaller in size compared to high-quality raster images, especially for graphics like logos, icons, and geometric shapes.

8. **Print Quality**: SVGs are resolution-independent, so they can be printed with high quality at any size.

Strengths

1. **Scalability**: Perfect for responsive Web design; images look sharp at any size or resolution.

2. **Editable**: Easily edited with text editors or vector graphic software.

3. **Performance**: Can reduce load times due to smaller file sizes compared to high-resolution raster images.

4. **Interactivity and Animation**: Offers dynamic and interactive capabilities, enhancing user experience.

5. **Accessibility and SEO Benefits**: Texts in SVGs are readable by screen readers and search engines.

Weaknesses

1. **Complexity for Detailed Images**: Not ideal for complex images like photographs; can become complex and large in file size.

2. **Browser Compatibility**: Some older browsers or specific features might have compatibility issues, although this is becoming less of a problem as people shift away from older browsers to newer browsers.

3. **Learning Curve**: Requires knowledge of XML and possibly CSS/JavaScript for advanced features.

4. **Security Concerns**: Being XML-based, SVG files can potentially contain harmful JavaScript, so they require careful handling and sanitization.

5. **Limited Editing Software**: While widely supported, not all graphic editing software are equally proficient at handling SVGs.

In summary, SVG is a powerful format for Web and graphic design, especially suited for logos, icons, and other designs that require scalability and interactivity. Its weaknesses are more apparent in handling complex images and require a bit of technical knowledge to fully utilize its capabilities.

USE CASES FOR SVG

The following prompt was supplied to Gemini in order to describe use cases for SVG in HTML Web pages.

```
Please describe significant use cases that involve SVG in
HTML Web pages, along with an explanation of the use cases.
```

```
Gemini:
SVG is a powerful tool in modern Web development, offering
precision, scalability, and flexibility for graphical
elements. Here are some significant use cases of SVG in
HTML Web pages, along with explanations for each:
```

1. High-Quality Scalable Icons and Logos

Use Case: Using SVG for icons, logos, and other vector graphics that need to retain high quality at any scale.

Explanation: Unlike raster images (like PNG or JPEG), SVGs are resolution-independent and remain crisp and clear at any size. This makes them ideal for logos and icons, especially in responsive designs where the image size adjusts to different screen resolutions.

2. Interactive and Animated Graphics

Use Case: Creating interactive diagrams, charts, and animations that respond to user actions.

Explanation: SVG can be manipulated with CSS and JavaScript, allowing for interactive and dynamic graphics. For instance, an SVG-based chart can be animated or updated in response to user inputs or data changes. This interactivity enhances user engagement and experience.

3. Complex Illustrations

Use Case: Embedding detailed illustrations and artwork that are zoomable without loss of quality.

Explanation: SVG is perfect for complex illustrations like technical diagrams, architectural plans, or detailed artwork. These graphics can be zoomed in on or scaled down while maintaining their quality, which is essential for conveying detailed information.

4. Data Visualization

Use Case: Creating dynamic data visualizations like graphs, pie charts, and maps.

Explanation: SVG's ability to scale and its support for interactivity make it suitable for data visualization. It can be used to create dynamic, data-driven charts and graphs that are both informative and visually appealing.

5. UI Elements and Controls

Use Case: Designing custom user interface elements like buttons, sliders, and progress bars.

Explanation: SVG provides more flexibility than traditional CSS in designing complex UI elements. With SVG, you can create detailed, scalable, and interactive UI components that enhance the user interface.

6. Text Manipulation and Accessibility

Use Case: Incorporating text within graphics that remains selectable and accessible.

Explanation: Texts in SVG are selectable and can be read by screen readers, unlike texts in raster images. This is particularly useful for accessibility and for scenarios where text and graphics need to work together, like in infographics.

7. Clipping and Masking Effects

Use Case: Applying complex clipping and masking effects to elements.

Explanation: SVG supports advanced clipping and masking capabilities, allowing for creative visual effects where parts of images or elements are hidden or revealed in specific shapes.

8. Web Typography and Decorative Text

Use Case: Creating artistic and decorative text effects.

Explanation: SVG offers extensive capabilities for stylizing and animating text, going beyond what CSS can achieve. This is useful for decorative purposes, such as fancy headings or stylized text in logos.

Conclusion

SVG's integration into HTML Web pages opens up a world of possibilities for high-quality graphics, interactive elements, and dynamic visualizations. Its strengths in scalability, interactivity, and precision make it an invaluable tool for creating engaging and effective Web content.

ACCESSIBILITY AND SVG

The following prompt was supplied to Gemini in order to describe the level of support for accessibility in SVG.

```
Please provide a detailed description of the level of
support for accessibility in SVG.
```

Gemini:

SVG offers a significant degree of support for accessibility, which is crucial for ensuring that Web content is available to all users, including those with disabilities. Here's a detailed description of the level of support for accessibility in SVG:

Semantic Structure

- **Descriptive Tags**: SVG allows the use of descriptive tags like `<title>` and `<desc>`, which can provide context or descriptions for screen readers. This is similar to providing `alt` text in HTML `<img>` elements.
- **Use of Text**: Unlike text in raster images, text in SVG is selectable and searchable, which is beneficial for screen readers and SEO.

ARIA (Accessible Rich Internet Applications) Integration

- **ARIA Roles and Properties**: SVG integrates well with ARIA roles and properties. ARIA attributes can be used within SVG to enhance the accessibility of SVG elements, particularly for dynamic or complex graphics.
- **Hidden Attribute**: The `aria-hidden` attribute can be used to hide decorative SVG elements from screen readers, focusing on the more content-relevant parts.

Keyboard Navigation

- **Focusable Elements**: SVG elements can be made focusable and navigable using keyboard navigation, which is essential for users who cannot use a mouse. The `tabindex` attribute can be used to include or exclude elements from the tab order.

Zoom and Scalability

- **Scalable Graphics**: One of the inherent advantages of SVG is its scalability. Users with visual impairments can zoom in without loss of quality, which is not possible with raster images.

Color and Contrast

- **Customization**: SVGs can be styled and manipulated with CSS. This means that colors and contrasts can be dynamically adjusted to meet various accessibility standards or user preferences.

Dynamic Updates

- **JavaScript Interaction**: SVGs can be dynamically updated with JavaScript, which means they can be made to reflect changes in real time. This is particularly useful for users relying on assistive technology to access up-to-date information.

Text Alternatives

- **Complex Images**: For complex SVG images like charts or graphs, providing a text alternative is crucial. This can be done using HTML elements alongside the SVG or within the SVG using tags like `<desc>`.

Assistive Technology Support

- **Compatibility**: Modern screen readers and assistive technologies generally support SVG. However, the level of support can vary, and keeping SVGs simple and well-structured improves accessibility.

Challenges and Considerations

- **Complexity**: Complex SVGs (like detailed graphs) can be challenging to make fully accessible. In such cases, providing textual descriptions or alternative content is important.
- **Browser and Assistive Technology Variability**: Different browsers and assistive technologies may interpret SVG accessibility features differently, so testing across various platforms is important.

Conclusion

SVG provides various features that support accessibility, making it a viable option for creating accessible Web graphics. Proper use of semantic elements, ARIA roles, and text alternatives, along with careful design considerations, can enhance the accessibility of SVG content. As with any Web technology, the key to effective accessibility in SVGs lies in thoughtful implementation and thorough testing across different devices and assistive technologies.

SECURITY ISSUES WITH SVG

The following prompt was supplied to Gemini in order to describe potential security issues with SVG.

```
Please provide a detailed description of potential security
issues involving SVG.
```

Gemini:

SVG is a powerful XML-based markup language for describing two-dimensional vector graphics. SVG is widely used on the Web due to its scalability and flexibility, but like many Web technologies, it comes with its own set of security considerations. Here's a detailed description of potential security issues involving SVG:

1. **Cross-Site Scripting (XSS) Attacks**
   - **Issue**: SVG files can contain JavaScript, which can be executed in the user's browser. If an SVG file is not properly sanitized and is allowed to include malicious scripts, it can lead to XSS attacks when the SVG is embedded in a Web page.
   - **Consequences**: This can allow attackers to steal cookies, session tokens, or even take over a user's session.

2. **Malicious Payloads**
   - **Issue**: SVG files can contain various types of potentially harmful content, including JavaScript, CSS, and even embedded raster images. This versatility makes it possible for SVG files to carry malicious payloads.
   - **Consequences**: If the SVG file is not properly validated and sanitized, it can be used to deliver various types of exploits.

3. **Phishing and Social Engineering**
   - **Issue**: SVGs can be crafted to look like legitimate interactive elements or familiar brands, tricking users into clicking on them or providing sensitive information.
   - **Consequences**: This can lead to phishing attacks where users are misled into giving away personal data or credentials.

4. **Resource Consumption**
   - **Issue**: SVGs can be designed to be computationally intensive to render, either intentionally or by accident.
   - **Consequences**: Loading complex SVGs can lead to significant performance hits on a user's device, potentially causing Denial of Service (DoS) like conditions.

5. **External Resource References**
   - **Issue**: SVGs can reference external resources, which can be used maliciously.
   - **Consequences**: This can lead to information leakage (through referrer headers), or the loading of malicious resources if the external resource is controlled by an attacker.

6. **Privacy Leaks**
   - **Issue**: SVGs can contain scripting or external resource references that send user data to remote servers without the user's knowledge.
   - **Consequences**: This can be a privacy concern, as it can be used to track users or collect sensitive information.

Mitigation Strategies
- **Content Sanitization**: Any SVG content uploaded by users should be properly sanitized to remove potentially malicious scripts or payloads.

This is especially important for Web applications that allow user-uploaded content.

• **CSP (Content Security Policy)**: Implementing a robust CSP can help prevent the execution of unauthorized scripts within SVGs.
• **Limiting SVG Features**: Restricting features like scripting, external resource loading, and embedding within SVGs can reduce the attack surface.
• **User Awareness and Education**: Educating users about the risks associated with unknown SVG files and encouraging caution can be an effective line of defense.

Conclusion

SVG, while being a versatile and powerful technology for Web graphics, brings its own set of security challenges. Awareness of these issues and implementing proper security measures and best practices are key to mitigating the risks associated with using SVG in Web applications.

SVG LINEAR GRADIENTS

The following prompt was supplied to Gemini in order to generate an HTML Web page that contains an SVG rectangle with a linear gradient.

Please generate an HTML Web page that contains a SVG rectangle of width 500 and height 300 that is rendered with an SVG linear gradient, along with an explanation of the code.

Gemini:
Here's how to create an SVG rectangle with a linear gradient, along with code explanations.

Listing 7.1 displays the contents of gemini_svg_linear_gradient. html that shows the code that Gemini generated in order to display a Web page that contains an SVG rectangle with linear gradient shading, an SVG polygon with radial gradient shading, and an SVG circle with radial gradient shading.

LISTING 7.1 gemini_svg_linear_gradient.html

```
<!DOCTYPE html>
<html lang="en">
<head>
    <meta charset="UTF-8">
    <meta name="viewport" content="width=device-width,
                                    initial-scale=1.0">
    <title>SVG Gradient Rectangle</title>
</head>
<body>
```

```
<svg width="500" height="300">
    <defs>
        <linearGradient id="myGradient" x1="0%" y1="0%"
                                        x2="100%" y2="0%">
            <stop offset="0%"
                    style="stop-color:rgb(255,0,0);" />
            <stop offset="100%"
                    style="stop-color:rgb(255,255,0);" />
        </linearGradient>
    </defs>
    <rect x="0" y="0" width="500" height="300"
                        fill="url(#myGradient)" />
</svg>
</body>
</html>
```

Explanation

The core of the code is the SVG structure itself. Let's break it down:

1. **`<svg>` Element:**
   - The `<svg>` tag defines the container for our SVG image. We set a `width` and `height` to determine its size.

2. **`<defs>` Element:**
   - The `<defs>` section is where we define reusable components within the SVG, like our gradient.

3. **`<linearGradient>` Element:**
   - Creates a linear gradient.
     - `id="myGradient"`: Assigns an ID so we can later use it to fill the rectangle.
     - `x1, y1, x2, y2`: Control the gradient direction (here, 0% to 100% on the x-axis creates a horizontal gradient).

4. **`<stop>` Elements:**
   - Define color points within the gradient.
     - `offset`: Position of the color transition (0% beginning, 100% end).
     - `style="stop-color: ...":` The color at that specific point within the gradient.

5. **`<rect>` Element:**
   - Draws our rectangle.
     - `x, y`: Set the rectangle's position (we use 0, 0 for the top-left corner).
     - `width, height`: Set the dimensions of the rectangle.
     - `fill="url(#myGradient)"`: Fills the rectangle with the gradient we defined.

Important:
   - **Embedding in HTML:** The SVG code is placed directly within the HTML `<body>` to render it on the Web page.

172 • CSS3 and SVG with Gemini

Experiment:

- Try changing the `stop-color` values for different gradient combinations.
- Modify the `x1`, `y1`, `x2`, `y2` attributes to generate gradients in various directions.

Launch the Web page `gemini_svg_rect_poly.html` by navigating to the directory that contains this HTML Web page and then typing the following command:

```
open gemini_svg_rect_poly.html
```

After a few moments you will see the Web page in Figure 7.1 that displays a snapshot of SVG-based graphics.

FIGURE 7.1. A Web page with SVG-based graphics.

SVG RADIAL GRADIENTS

The following prompt was supplied to Gemini in order to generate an HTML Web page that contains an SVG rectangle with a radial gradient.

Please generate an HTML Web page that contains an SVG rectangle of width 500 and height 300 that is rendered with an SVG radial gradient, along with an explanation of the code.

Gemini:
Absolutely! Here's the HTML page containing the SVG rectangle with a radial gradient, along with a breakdown of the code.

Listing 7.2 displays the contents of `Gemini_svg_radial_gradient.html` that shows the code that Gemini generated in order to display a Web page that contains an SVG rectangle with radial gradient shading.

LISTING 7.2 gemini_svg_radial_gradient.html

```
<!DOCTYPE html>
<html lang="en">
<head>
    <meta charset="UTF-8">
    <meta name="viewport" content="width=device-width,
                                    initial-scale=1.0">
    <title>SVG Radial Gradient Rectangle</title>
</head>
<body>
    <svg width="500" height="300">
        <defs>
            <radialGradient id="myRadialGradient" cx="50%"
                                    cy="50%" r="50%">
                <stop offset="0%"
                        style="stop-color:rgb(255,0,0);" />
                <stop offset="100%"
                        style="stop-color:rgb(0,0,255);" />
            </radialGradient>
        </defs>
        <rect x="0" y="0" width="500" height="300"
                        fill="url(#myRadialGradient)" />
    </svg>
</body>
</html>
```

Explanation

Let's see how this code is similar and different from the linear gradient example:

1. **`<svg>` and `<rect>`:** These elements remain the same, defining the SVG canvas and the actual rectangle shape.

2. **`<defs>`:** Still serves as the container for our reusable definition of the gradient.

3. **`<radialGradient>`**
   - This element replaces `<linearGradient>`. Here's how the attributes work:
     - `id="myRadialGradient"`: A unique identifier to reference the gradient.
     - `cx`, `cy`: Define the center point of the gradient (50%, 50% places it in the middle).
     - `r`: Sets the radius of the gradient's outer circle (50% extends to the edges of the rectangle).

4. **<stop> elements:**
   - Their function is the same—defining color points and their positions (offset) within the gradient.
5. **fill="url(#myRadialGradient)":** Like before, this fills the rectangle with our defined gradient.

Customization:

- **Colors:** Play with the stop-color values within the <stop> elements to experiment with different colors.
- **Center and Radius:** Change cx, cy, and r values to shift the center point of the gradient and alter its coverage area.
- **Additional Stops:** Explore creating more complex gradients by adding more <stop> elements.

Launch the Web page gemini_svg_radial_gradient.html by navigating to the directory that contains this HTML Web page and then typing the following command:

```
open gemini_svg_radial_gradient.html
```

After a few moments you will see the Web page in Figure 7.2 that displays a rectangle rendered with a radial gradient.

FIGURE 7.2. A rectangle with a radial gradient.

A TRIANGLE WITH A RADIAL GRADIENT

The following prompt was supplied to Gemini in order to generate SVG code for a triangle that is rendered with a radial gradient in an HTML Web page.

```
Please generate an HTML Web page that contains a triangle
with width 200 and height 400 that is rendered with
a radial gradient and a drop shadow, along with an
explanation of the code.
```

```
Gemini:
Here's how you can create that along with explanations.
Note that drawing triangles directly in SVG requires using
the <polygon> element.
```

LISTING 7.3 triangleRG1.html

```html
<!DOCTYPE html>
<html lang="en">
<head>
    <meta charset="UTF-8">
    <meta name="viewport" content="width=device-width,
                                initial-scale=1.0">
    <title>Gradient Triangle</title>
    <style>
        svg {
            filter: drop-shadow(5px 8px 10px
                                rgba(0,0,0,0.5));
        }
    </style>
</head>
<body>
    <svg width="300" height="500">
        <defs>
            <radialGradient id="triangleGradient" cx="50%"
                                cy="25%" r="70%">
                <stop offset="0%"
                            style="stop-color:yellow;" />
                <stop offset="100%"
                            style="stop-color:orange;" />
            </radialGradient>
        </defs>

        <polygon points="150,20 30,420 270,420"
                        fill="url(#triangleGradient)" />
    </svg>
</body>
</html>
```

Explanation:

SVG Structure

- **<svg>:** The container for our SVG graphic. Extra width and height were added for the drop shadow.
- **<defs>:** Holds the definition of our radial gradient (triangleGradient).
- **<radialGradient>:** Similar to previous examples, it defines our gradient properties (center, radius, colors).
- **<polygon>:** The element used to draw a triangle.
  - points: Defines the triangle's coordinates. For an isosceles triangle centered at the top:
    - (150, 20): Top vertex
    - (30, 420): Bottom-left vertex
    - (270, 420): Bottom-right vertex

CSS

- svg { filter: drop-shadow(...) }: Applies a drop shadow to the entire SVG element. Adjust the values to your liking:
  - 5px 8px: Horizontal and vertical offset of the shadow.
  - 10px: Blur radius of the shadow.
  - rgba(0,0,0,0.5): Shadow color with an alpha value for semitransparency.

Customization:

- **Triangle Shape:** Modify the points attribute of the polygon to change the triangle's shape.
- **Gradient:** Tweak the gradient colors, center, and radius within the <radialGradient> element.
- **Shadow:** Change the filter's drop-shadow values to tweak the shadow's appearance.

Important Note: Modern browsers support these features well, but if you need to target very old browsers, you might consider alternate ways to simulate shadows.

Launch the Web page gemini_svg_triangle.html by navigating to the directory that contains this HTML Web page and then typing the following command:

```
open gemini_svg_triangle.html
```

After a few moments you will see the image in Figure 7.3 that displays a triangle with a radial gradient.

FIGURE 7.3. An SVG triangle with a radial gradient.

SVG 2D SHAPES AND GRADIENTS

The following prompt was supplied to Gemini in order to generate an HTML Web page that contains several SVG-based elements.

Please generate an HTML Web page that contains an SVG triangle, SVG circle, SVG ellipse, and an 8-sided SVG polygon that are rendered with either a linear gradient or a radial gradient, along with an explanation of the code.

Gemini:
Here's a breakdown of the HTML page containing the shapes and gradients, along with explanations.

Listing 7.4 displays the contents of gemini_svg_2d_shapes.html that shows the code that Gemini generated in order to display a Web page that contains an SVG rectangle with linear gradient shading, an SVG polygon with radial gradient shading, and an SVG circle with radial gradient shading.

LISTING 7.4 gemini_svg_2d_shapes.html

```
<!DOCTYPE html>
<html lang="en">
<head>
    <meta charset="UTF-8">
    <meta name="viewport" content="width=device-width,
                                   initial-scale=1.0">
    <title>SVG Shapes and Gradients</title>
</head>
<body>
    <svg width="600" height="500">
        <defs>
```

```
<linearGradient id="linearGrad" x1="0%"
                  y1="50%" x2="100%" y2="50%">
   <stop offset="0%" style="stop-color:purple;" />
   <stop offset="100%" style="stop-color:blue;" />
</linearGradient>

<radialGradient id="radialGrad" cx="50%"
                    cy="50%" r="50%">
   <stop offset="0%" style="stop-color:yellow;" />
   <stop offset="100%" style="stop-color:green;" />
</radialGradient>
</defs>

<polygon points="50,20 150,120 50,220"
                    fill="url(#linearGrad)" />

<circle cx="250" cy="100" r="80"
                    fill="url(#radialGrad)" />

<ellipse cx="400" cy="180" rx="100" ry="60"
                    fill="url(#linearGrad)" />

<polygon points="380,320 425,280 495,280 540,320
                  540,390 495,430 425,430 380,390"
                    fill="url(#radialGrad)" />
    </svg>
</body>
</html>
```

Explanation

- **<svg>:** The core container for our SVG elements.
- **<defs>**
  - Holds two reusable gradients:
    - linearGrad: A simple purple-to-blue linear gradient going horizontally.
    - radialGrad: A yellow-to-green radial gradient.
- **Shapes**
  - **<polygon>** Creates our triangle. The points attribute defines the coordinates of each vertex.
  - **<circle>** Defines a circle with attributes controlling its center (cx, cy) and radius (r).
  - **<ellipse>** Draws an ellipse with center (cx, cy), horizontal radius (rx), and vertical radius (ry).
  - **Another <polygon>** We construct an octagon by carefully specifying the points attribute for its eight vertices.
- **fill="url(#...)"** Each shape references either linearGrad or radialGrad from the <defs> section to fill itself with the gradient.

Let's Customize

- **Gradient Tweaks:** Modify the colors (stop-color) and other parameters within the gradients in the <defs> section.
- **Shape Experimentation:** Try different attributes to change the size and positions of the shapes.
- **Add more Shapes:** Explore the creation of rectangles (<rect>), lines (<line>), and paths (<path>) and try applying gradients to them.

Launch the Web page gemini_svg_2d_shapes.html in Listing 7.4 by navigating to the directory that contains this HTML Web page and then typing the following command:

```
open gemini_svg_2d_shapes.html
```

After a few moments, you will see the contents of Figure 7.4 that displays a triangle, circle, ellipse, and polygon with gradient shading.

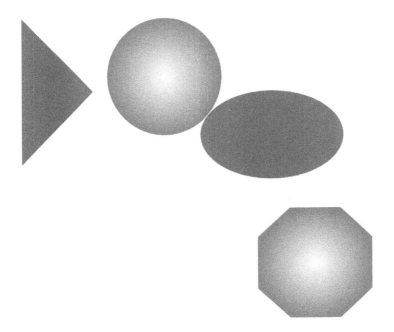

FIGURE 7.4. SVG-based 2D shapes.

SVG QUADRATIC BEZIER CURVES

The following prompt was supplied to Gemini in order to create an HTML Web page that contains fifty random SVG quadratic Bezier curves.

```
Please generate an HTML Web page that contains a set of
fifty random SVG quadratic Bezier curves with a fill
```

pattern alternating between two different radial gradients, with a maximum width of 600 and a maximum height of 400, along with an explanation of the code.

Gemini:
Absolutely! Here's the HTML file with embedded SVG and the accompanying explanation. Save this code as an HTML file (e.g., "curves.html") and open it in your browser to see the result.

Listing 7.5 displays the contents of the Python file gemini_svg_random_ quadratic_bezier_curves.py that generates an SVG document that contains randomly generated quadratic Bezier curves.

LISTING 7.5 gemini_svg_random_quadratic_bezier_curves.html

```
<!DOCTYPE html>
<html lang="en">
<head>
    <meta charset="UTF-8">
    <meta name="viewport" content="width=device-width,
                                    initial-scale=1.0">
    <title>Random Quadratic Bezier Curves</title>
    <style>
        body {
            margin: 0; /* Remove default body margins */
        }
        svg {
            background-color: #f0f0f0;
                /* Background for the whole SVG canvas */
            width: 100%;
            height: 100vh;
            /* Make the SVG take up the full viewport height */
        }
    </style>
</head>
<body>

    <svg viewBox="0 0 600 400">
        <defs>
            <radialGradient id="gradient1" cx="50%"
                                    cy="50%" r="50%">
                <stop offset="0%" stop-color="orange" />
                <stop offset="100%" stop-color="red" />
            </radialGradient>
            <radialGradient id="gradient2" cx="50%"
                                    cy="50%" r="50%">
                <stop offset="0%" stop-color="lightblue" />
                <stop offset="100%" stop-color="blue" />
            </radialGradient>
        </defs>
```

```
<script>
    for (let i = 0; i < 50; i++) {
        let path = document.
createElementNS('http://www.w3.org/2000/svg', 'path');
        let startX = Math.random() * 600;
        let startY = Math.random() * 400;
        let controlX = Math.random() * 600;
        let controlY = Math.random() * 400;
        let endX = Math.random() * 600;
        let endY = Math.random() * 400;

        let d = 'M ${startX},${startY} Q
            ${controlX},${controlY} ${endX},${endY}';
        path.setAttribute('d', d);

        path.setAttribute('fill', i % 2 === 0 ?
            'url(#gradient1)' : 'url(#gradient2)');
        path.setAttribute('stroke', 'black');
        path.setAttribute('stroke-width', 2);

        document.querySelector('svg').
                                appendChild(path);
    }
    </script>
    </svg>

</body>
</html>
```

Code Explanation:

Basic HTML Structure: Sets up the basic document structure.

CSS Styling:
    body: Removes default margins.
    svg: Provides background color, makes it fill the screen width, and uses viewport height (vh) for responsiveness.

SVG <defs> Section:
    Defines two radial gradients ("gradient1" and "gradient2") with color stops for the alternating fill patterns. Notice the id attributes so we can reference them later.

JavaScript loop:
    Iterates fifty times to create fifty curves.
    createElementNS: Creates an SVG <path> element.

Generates random coordinates for the start point (startX, startY), control point (controlX, controlY), and end point (endX, endY).

d attribute: Constructs the quadratic Bezier curve path string using the Q command.

setAttribute:

Sets the fill to alternate between gradients, using url(#gradient1) and url(#gradient2).

Adds a black stroke and sets the line width.

document.querySelector('svg').appendChild(path): Adds the generated <path> to the SVG.

Launch the HTML Web page from the command line as follows:

```
open gemini_svg_random_quadratic_bezier_curves.html
```

After a few moments you will see the image (or something similar) that is displayed in Figure 7.5.

FIGURE 7.5. SVG-based quadratic Bezier curves.

SVG CUBIC BEZIER CURVES

The following prompt was supplied to Gemini in order to create an HTML Web page that contains fifty random SVG cubic Bezier curves.

Please generate an HTML Web page that contains a set of fifty random SVG cubic Bezier curves with a fill pattern alternating between two different radial gradients, with a maximum width of 600 and a maximum height of 400, along with an explanation of the code.

Gemini:
Absolutely! Here's the HTML code for generating random SVG
cubic Bézier curves, similar to the previous example.

Listing 7.6 displays the contents of gemini_svg_cubic_bezier_curves.
html that generates an SVG document that contains randomly generated
cubic Bezier curves.

LISTING 7.6 gemini_svg_random_cubic_bezier_curves.html

```html
<!DOCTYPE html>
<html lang="en">
<head>
    <meta charset="UTF-8">
    <meta name="viewport" content="width=device-width,
                                    initial-scale=1.0">
    <title>Random Cubic Bezier Curves</title>
    <style>
        body {
            margin: 0;
        }
        svg {
            background-color: #f0f0f0;
            width: 100%;
            height: 100vh;
        }
    </style>
</head>
<body>

    <svg viewBox="0 0 600 400">
        <defs>
            <radialGradient id="gradient1" cx="50%"
                                           cy="50%" r="50%">
                <stop offset="0%" stop-color="lightgreen" />
                <stop offset="100%" stop-color="green" />
            </radialGradient>
            <radialGradient id="gradient2" cx="50%"
                                           cy="50%" r="50%">
                <stop offset="0%" stop-color="yellow" />
                <stop offset="100%" stop-color="gold" />
            </radialGradient>
        </defs>

        <script>
            for (let i = 0; i < 50; i++) {
                let path = document.
    createElementNS('http://www.w3.org/2000/svg', 'path');
                let startX = Math.random() * 600;
                let startY = Math.random() * 400;
```

```
let controlX1 = Math.random() * 600;
let controlY1 = Math.random() * 400;
let controlX2 = Math.random() * 600;
let controlY2 = Math.random() * 400;
let endX = Math.random() * 600;
let endY = Math.random() * 400;

let d = 'M ${startX},${startY} C
${controlX1},${controlY1} ${controlX2},${controlY2}
                        ${endX},${endY}';
path.setAttribute('d', d);

path.setAttribute('fill', i % 2 === 0 ?
    'url(#gradient1)' : 'url(#gradient2)');
path.setAttribute('stroke', 'black');
path.setAttribute('stroke-width', 2);

document.querySelector('svg').
                        appendChild(path);
        }
    </script>
</svg>

</body>
</html>
```

Explanation of Changes

Cubic Bézier Curve Syntax: The main difference is in the d attribute for the <path>. Here we use the 'C' command for cubic Bézier curves, requiring two control points (controlX1, controlY1), (controlX2, controlY2) along with the end point.

Colors: I've adjusted the gradients to use green/yellow variations for a different visual effect.

Key Points:

Both quadratic ('Q') and cubic ('C') Bézier curves allow vast flexibility in shapes. Cubic curves offer finer control due to the additional control point.

You can easily customize the colors, number of curves, and so on, within the code.

Launch the HTML Web page in Listing 7.6 from the command line as follows:

```
open gemini_svg_random_cubic_bezier_curves.html
```

After a few moments you will see the image (or something similar) that is displayed in Figure 7.6.

FIGURE 7.6. SVG-based cubic Bezier curves.

SVG AND 2D TRANSFORMS

The following prompt was supplied to Gemini in order to generate SVG-based 2D transformation effects.

Please generate an HTML Web page that contains an SVG-based rectangle with animated rotation, an SVG triangle with an animated skew effect, an SVG polygon with animated scaling effect, and an SVG-based ellipse with an animated rotation and also an animated scaling effect, along with an explanation of the SVG code.

Gemini:
Here's a breakdown of the HTML, SVG, and CSS to achieve the animated SVG shapes you described.

Listing 7.7 displays the contents of gemini_svg_2d_transforms.html that contains Gemini-generated SVG code that performs 2D transform-based animation effects on four 2D shapes.

LISTING 7.7 gemini_svg_2d_transforms.html

```
<!DOCTYPE html>
<html lang="en">
<head>
    <meta charset="UTF-8">
    <meta name="viewport" content="width=device-width,
                                   initial-scale=1.0">
```

```
    <title>Animated SVG Shapes</title>
    <style>
        svg {
            width: 600px;
            height: 400px;
            display: block;
            margin: 30px auto;
        }
    </style>
</head>
<body>
    <svg>
        <rect id="rotating-rect" x="50" y="50" width="100"
                            height="50" fill="orange" />

        <polygon id="skewing-triangle"
            points="250,50 300,150 200,150" fill="purple"/>

        <ellipse id="scaling-ellipse" cx="400" cy="150"
                            rx="60" ry="30" fill="teal" />

        <polygon id="scaling-polygon"
                    points="280,250 325,210 395,210 440,250
                        440,320 395,360 325,360 280,320"
fill="tomato" />

        <animateTransform
            attributeName="transform"
            attributeType="XML"
            type="rotate"
            from="0 75 75"
            to="360 75 75"
            dur="3s"
            repeatCount="indefinite" />

        <animateTransform
            attributeName="transform"
            attributeType="XML"
            type="skewX"
            from="0"
            to="45"
            dur="2s"
            repeatCount="indefinite"
            additive="sum" />

        <animateTransform
            attributeName="transform"
            attributeType="XML"
            type="scale"
            from="1 1"
            to="1.3 0.8"
            dur="2.5s"
```

```
            repeatCount="indefinite"
            additive="sum" />

        <animateTransform
            attributeName="transform"
            attributeType="XML"
            type="rotate"
            from="0 400 150"
            to="360 400 150"
            dur="4s"
            repeatCount="indefinite" />
    </svg>
</body>
</html>
```

Explanation

- **SVG Structure:**
  - Several SVG shapes: `<rect>`, `<polygon>`, `<ellipse>`, with unique IDs that we'll use for targeting the animations.
- **`<animateTransform>` Elements**
  - These elements are what bring your shapes to life. Let's break down some common attributes:
    - `attributeName="transform"`: We are animating transform properties.
    - `attributeType="XML"`: Specifies we are dealing with XML attributes.
    - `type`: The specific transform (`rotate`, `skewX`, `scale`).
    - `from`, `to`: Start and end values of the animation.
    - `dur`: Duration in seconds.
    - `repeatCount="indefinite"`: Makes the animation loop forever.
- **Key Notes:**
  - **Multiple Transforms:** The ellipse has both a scaling animation and a separate rotation animation applied simultaneously.
  - **`additive="sum"`:** Makes animations build upon their previous state smoothly instead of abruptly resetting.

Let's Customize

- **Colors:** Play with the `fill` attribute of your shapes.
- **Animation Speeds:** Adjust the `dur` (duration) of the animations.
- **Transformations:** Try `skewY`, `translate`, or chain together multiple transform types within one `<animateTransform>`.

Launch the Web page `gemini_svg_2d_transforms.html` by navigating to the directory that contains Listing 7.7 and then typing the following command:

```
open gemini_svg_2d_transforms.html
```

After a few moments you will see the image in Figure 7.7 that displays a snapshot of SVG-based animation of various polygonal shapes.

FIGURE 7.7. SVG-based animation with polygonal shapes.

ANIMATED SVG CUBIC BEZIER CURVES

The following prompt was supplied to Gemini in order to generate animation effects with cubic Bezier curves.

Please generate an HTML Web page that contains an animation effect involving fifty random cubic Bezier curves.

Gemini:
Absolutely! It seems there might be a small oversight in the previous example. Here's the corrected version, along with explanations about the potential fixes.

Listing 7.8 displays gemini_svg_animated_bezier_curves.html that generates an SVG document that contains randomly generated quadratic Bezier curves.

LISTING 7.8 gemini_svg_animated_cubic_bezier_curves.html

```
<!DOCTYPE html>
<html lang="en">
<head>
    <meta charset="UTF-8">
    <meta name="viewport" content="width=device-width,
                                    initial-scale=1.0">
```

```
<title>Animated Bezier Curves</title>
<style>
    body {
        margin: 0;
    }
    svg {
        background-color: #f0f0f0;
        width: 100%;
        height: 100vh;
    }
</style>
</head>
<body>

    <svg viewBox="0 0 600 400">
        <defs>
            <radialGradient id="gradient1" cx="50%"
                                      cy="50%" r="50%">
                <stop offset="0%" stop-color="lightblue" />
                <stop offset="100%" stop-color="blue" />
            </radialGradient>
            <radialGradient id="gradient2" cx="50%"
                                      cy="50%" r="50%">
                <stop offset="0%" stop-color="orange" />
                <stop offset="100%" stop-color="red" />
            </radialGradient>
        </defs>
    </svg>

    <script>
        const svg = document.querySelector('svg');
        const paths = [];

        function createPaths() {
            for (let i = 0; i < 50; i++) {
                let path = document.
    createElementNS('http://www.w3.org/2000/svg', 'path');
                paths.push(path);
                svg.appendChild(path);
                generatePathData(path);
                            // Initial curve generation
                path.setAttribute('fill', i % 2 === 0 ?
                    'url(#gradient1)' : 'url(#gradient2)');
                path.setAttribute('stroke', 'black');
                path.setAttribute('stroke-width', 2);
            }
        }

        function generatePathData(path) {
            let startX = Math.random() * 600;
            let startY = Math.random() * 400;
```

```
        let controlX1 = Math.random() * 600;
        let controlY1 = Math.random() * 400;
        let controlX2 = Math.random() * 600;
        let controlY2 = Math.random() * 400;
        let endX = Math.random() * 600;
        let endY = Math.random() * 400;

        let d = 'M ${startX},${startY} C
    ${controlX1},${controlY1} ${controlX2},${controlY2}
                                    ${endX},${endY}';
        path.setAttribute('d', d);
    }

    function animate() {
        paths.forEach(path => generatePathData(path));
        requestAnimationFrame(animate);
    }

    createPaths(); // Create the paths initially
    animate();
    </script>
</body>
</html>
```

Explanation:

- **SVG Versus CSS:** We'll animate the "d" attribute of SVG `<path>` elements for direct control over the Bezier curves.
- **curves Array:** Stores references to our SVG curve elements.
- **animate() Function:** Uses `requestAnimationFrame` to create a smooth animation loop. Inside the loop, we'll update each curve's path.
- **Helper Functions:**
  - `setInitialCurveProperties`: Handles the initial setup (position, color, etc.) of each curve.
  - `updateCurvePath`: **Core of the animation.** Here you'll change the control points of the Bezier curve to achieve the desired effect.
  - `generateBezierPath`: Constructs your cubic Bezier curve strings.

Animation Types (Ideas)

1. **Organic Morphing:** Gradually tweak all control points of each curve, achieving a fluid morphing effect.

2. **Wave-Like Motion:** Adjust control points in a pattern across the curves to simulate a ripple or wave.

3. **Particle-Like:** Combine changes in path, size, and opacity to simulate particles dispersing or gathering.

Customization is key. The magic lies in how you write your `updateCurvePath` and `generateBezierPath` functions.

Launch the HTML Web page in Listing 7.8 from the command line as follows:

```
open gemini_svg_animated_cubic_bezier_curves.html
```

After a few moments you will see the image in Figure 7.8 that displays a snapshot of SVG-based animation of multiple cubic Bezier curves.

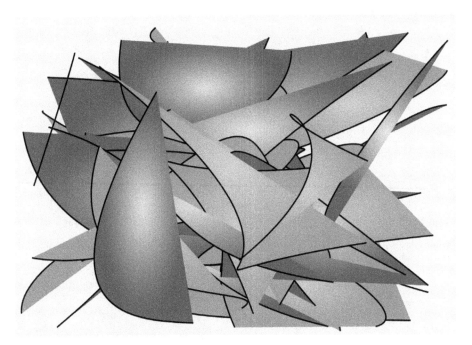

FIGURE 7.8. SVG-based animation of multiple cubic Bezier curves.

HOVER EFFECTS

The following prompt was supplied to Gemini in order to generate an HTML Web page that contains SVG and a hover animation effect.

```
Please generate an HTML Web page with a 300x300 SVG
rectangle that has a rotating animation effect on a hover
event.
```

```
Gemini:
Absolutely! Here's an example of a hover effect with SVG
inside an HTML Web page.
```

LISTING 7.9 gemini_svg_hover.html

```
<!DOCTYPE html>
<html lang="en">
<head>
    <meta charset="UTF-8">
    <meta name="viewport" content="width=device-width,
                                 initial-scale=1.0">
    <title>Rotating Rectangle</title>
    <style>
        .rectangle-container {
            width: 300px;
            height: 300px;
            margin: 50px auto;
        }

        .rectangle {
            width: 100%;
            height: 100%;
            fill: lightblue;
            transform-origin: 50% 50%;
                            /* Rotate around center */
            transition: transform 0.5s ease-in-out;
                            /* Smooth animation */
        }

        .rectangle-container:hover .rectangle {
            transform: rotate(180deg);
        }
    </style>
</head>
<body>
    <div class="rectangle-container">
        <svg viewBox="0 0 300 300">
            <rect class="rectangle" x="0" y="0"/>
        </svg>
    </div>
</body>
</html>
```

Launch the Web page gemini_svg_hover.html by navigating to the directory that contains this HTML Web page and then typing the following command:

```
open gemini_svg_hover.html
```

After a few moments you will see the image in Figure 7.9 that displays a snapshot of a SVG-based hover effect.

FIGURE 7.9. SVG-based hover effect.

SVG VERSUS CSS3: A COMPARISON

The following prompt was supplied to Gemini in order to describe scenarios where it's better to use SVG instead of CSS3, as well as scenarios where it's better to use CSS3 instead of SVG.

Please provide a detailed comparison of SVG and CSS3, along
with scenarios where it's better to use SVG instead of
CSS3, and scenarios where it's better to use CSS3 instead
of SVG.

Gemini:
SVG and Cascading Style Sheets Level 3 (CSS3) are both
essential tools in modern Web design, but they serve
different purposes and have unique characteristics.
Understanding their differences can guide you in choosing
the right tool for specific scenarios.

SVG

Nature and Use:

- SVG is an XML-based image format used to define vector-based graphics for the Web.
- It allows for the creation of complex graphics including paths, shapes, text, and embedded raster graphics.

Key Features:

- **Scalability**: SVG images can be scaled to any size without loss of quality, making them ideal for responsive design.
- **Manipulation**: SVG elements can be manipulated via CSS and JavaScript.
- **Interactivity**: Supports user interactions and animations.
- **Accessibility**: Texts within SVGs are selectable and searchable, beneficial for accessibility and SEO.

CSS3 (Cascading Style Sheets Level 3)

Nature and Use:

- CSS3 is a style sheet language used for describing the presentation of a document written in a markup language like HTML.
- It's primarily used for styling and laying out Web pages.

Key Features:

- **Advanced Styling**: Includes advanced properties for text effects, box models, animations, transitions, and transforms.
- **Responsiveness**: CSS3 has features like media queries for responsive Web design.
- **Browser Compatibility**: Widely supported across modern Web browsers.

Scenarios for Using SVG over CSS3

1. **Complex Shapes and Icons**: SVG is more suited for detailed and complex shapes like logos and icons that need to scale without losing quality.
2. **Graphs and Charts**: For interactive and dynamic charts where scalability and precise rendering are crucial.
3. **Illustrations and Artwork**: Detailed illustrations and artistic elements are best created with SVG.
4. **Interactive Graphics**: SVG's ability to integrate with JavaScript makes it ideal for graphics requiring interactivity.
5. **Text Inside Images**: If you need selectable and searchable text within your images.

Scenarios for Using CSS3 over SVG

1. **Styling Web Content**: CSS3 is the standard for styling and laying out Web pages, including typography, color schemes, and spacing.
2. **Simple Animations and Transitions**: For basic animations like hover effects, transitions, and transformations on HTML elements.
3. **Responsive Layouts**: CSS3's media queries are essential for creating responsive designs that adjust to different screen sizes.
4. **Performance**: For basic shapes and effects, CSS3 can be less resource-intensive than SVG.

5. **Browser Rendering**: While SVG is widely supported, some complex SVG graphics can have compatibility issues in older browsers, whereas CSS3 properties often have fallback options.

Conclusion

- **Use SVG** when dealing with complex, scalable vector graphics, interactive elements, and when image quality is a priority.
- **Use CSS3** for styling, simple animations, responsive layout design, and when working with standard Web content.

By understanding the strengths and limitations of both SVG and CSS3, you can make more informed decisions about which tool to use for specific design requirements.

SVG VERSUS PNG: A COMPARISON

The following prompt was supplied to Gemini in order to describe scenarios where it's better to use SVG instead of PNG, as well as scenarios where it's better to use PNG instead of SVG.

Please provide a detailed comparison of SVG and PNG, along with scenarios where it's better to use SVG instead of PNG, and scenarios where it's better to use PNG instead of SVG.

Gemini:
SVG and PNG (Portable Network Graphics) are both popular image formats used on the Web, each with its own strengths and ideal use cases. Here's a detailed comparison of the two, along with scenarios where one might be preferred over the other.

SVG

Nature: SVG is a vector image format. It uses mathematical equations to define the graphics, such as shapes, lines, and colors.

File Size: SVG files are often smaller, especially for simpler designs. Their size doesn't increase with the complexity of the image.

Scalability: Being vector-based, SVG images can be scaled to any size without loss of quality.

Manipulation: SVG can be manipulated and animated using CSS and JavaScript.

Interactivity: SVG supports interactivity and dynamic updates, making it suitable for interactive Web applications.

Accessibility: Text in SVG images is selectable and searchable, which is better for accessibility and SEO.

Browser Rendering: SVGs are rendered by the browser, making them resolution-independent and always crisp.

PNG (Portable Network Graphics)

Nature: PNG is a raster (or bitmap) image format. It represents images in a grid of pixels.

File Size: File size increases with the resolution and color depth. PNGs can be larger for high-resolution images.

Scalability: Scaling up can lead to loss of quality (pixelation), while scaling down is generally fine.

Manipulation: Cannot be easily manipulated or animated like SVG. Requires image editing software for any changes.

Interactivity: PNGs do not support interactivity or dynamic changes.

Transparency: Supports transparency, which is useful for overlays, logos, and Web graphics.

Image Quality: Excellent for complex images like photographs due to its support for high color depths and lossless compression.

When to Use SVG

1. **Logos and Icons**: For scalable graphics that need to stay sharp at any size.
2. **Graphs and Charts**: For interactive and dynamic data visualizations.
3. **Responsive Web Design**: In designs that need to adapt to various screen sizes.
4. **Simple Animations**: For graphics that require basic animations or transitions.
5. **Web Applications**: Where interactivity and dynamic updates to the graphic elements are necessary.

When to Use PNG

1. **Photographs**: For complex images with subtle color variations, like photos.
2. **Images with Transparency**: For graphics that require a transparent background.
3. **Detailed Imagery**: When image details must remain exact at a specific resolution.
4. **Print Materials**: For high-quality print documents where image clarity is crucial and resizing is not required.
5. **Compatibility**: When absolute compatibility with older systems or browsers is necessary.

Conclusion

- **Use SVG** for graphics that need scalability, interactivity, and are generally simpler in color composition (like logos, icons, charts).
- **Use PNG** for static images where color depth and detail are important, like photographs, or when transparency is required.

Both formats have their place in Web design and development, and the choice often depends on the specific needs of the project regarding scalability, image complexity, and interactivity.

SVG FILTERS

As you know from the previous chapter, filter effects can significantly enhance the visual experience of the contents of an HTML Web page. In Chapter 3 you learned about CSS3 filters, and in this chapter, you will learn about SVG Filters, as shown in the following list:

* `<feBlend>` - filter for combining images
* `<feColorMatrix>` - filter for color transforms
* `<feComponentTransfer>`
* `<feComposite>`
* `<feConvolveMatrix>`
* `<feDiffuseLighting>`
* `<feDisplacementMap>`
* `<feFlood>`
* `<feGaussianBlur>`
* `<feTurbulence>`

The following subsections contain examples of some of the filters in the preceding bullet list of filters.

SVG BLUR FILTER

The following prompt was supplied to Gemini in order to generate an HTML Web page with an SVG blur filter.

Please generate an HTML Web page that contains a rectangle that is rendered with an SVG blur filter, along with an explanation of the code.

Gemini:
Absolutely! Here's an example of displaying a rectangle with an SVG blur filter.

Listing 7.10 displays the contents of gemini_svg_blur_filter.html that contains Gemini-generated SVG rectangle with a blur filter effect.

LISTING 7.10 gemini_svg_blur1.html

```
<!DOCTYPE html>
<html lang="en">
<head>
    <meta charset="UTF-8">
    <meta name="viewport" content="width=device-width,
                                initial-scale=1.0">
```

```
<title>Blurred Rectangle</title>
<style>
    svg {
        width: 300px;
        height: 200px;
    }
</style>
</head>
<body>
    <svg>
        <defs>
            <filter id="rectangleBlur">
                <feGaussianBlur stdDeviation="5" />
            </filter>
        </defs>

        <rect x="20" y="20" width="250" height="150"
fill="skyblue" filter="url(#rectangleBlur)" />
    </svg>
</body>
</html>
```

Explanation

- **<svg>:** The container for our shape and graphic effects.
- **<defs>:** The definitions section where we will place our filter.
- **<filter>:**
  - id="rectangleBlur": Gives the filter a unique identifier.
  - <feGaussianBlur>: The specific filter element responsible for the Gaussian blur effect.
    - stdDeviation="5": Controls the intensity of the blur. Higher values mean a stronger blur.
- **<rect>:** Our rectangle shape.
  - filter="url(#rectangleBlur)": Applies the filter we defined earlier by referencing its ID.

Important Notes

- **Browser Support:** SVG filters are well supported across modern browsers.
- **Filter Complexity:** SVG filters can be much more complex, involving multiple filter primitives combined for various effects.

Customization

- **Blur Intensity:** Play around with the stdDeviation attribute of the <feGaussianBlur>.
- **Different Filters:** Explore other SVG filter primitives like feColorMatrix, feOffset, and more from the SVG filter documentation: https://developer.mozilla.org/en-US/docs/Web/SVG/Element/filter

Launch the Web page gemini_svg_blur1.html by navigating to the directory that contains this HTML Web page and then typing the following command:

```
open gemini_svg_blur1.html
```

After a few moments you will see an SVG rectangle rendered with an SVG blur filter, as shown in Figure 7.10.

FIGURE 7.10. An SVG rectangle with a blur filter.

SVG TURBULENCE FILTER

The following prompt was supplied to Gemini in order to generate an HTML Web page with an SVG turbulence filter.

Please generate an HTML Web page that contains a rectangle that is rendered with an SVG turbulence filter, along with an explanation of the code.

Gemini:
Here's the code and explanation for applying an SVG turbulence filter to a rectangle.

Listing 7.11 displays the contents of gemini_svg_turbulence_filter. html that contains Gemini-generated SVG rectangle with a blur filter effect.

LISTING 7.11 gemini_svg_turbulence1.html

```
<!DOCTYPE html>
<html lang="en">
<head>
    <meta charset="UTF-8">
    <meta name="viewport" content="width=device-width,
                                   initial-scale=1.0">
    <title>Turbulent Rectangle</title>
```

```
<style>
    svg {
        width: 300px;
        height: 200px;
    }
</style>
</head>
<body>
    <svg>
        <defs>
            <filter id="turbulenceFilter">
                <feTurbulence type="turbulence"
baseFrequency="0.05" numOctaves="2"
result="turbulenceOutput" />
                    <feDisplacementMap in2="turbulenceOutput"
                                        in="SourceGraphic"
                                        scale="30"
xChannelSelector="R" yChannelSelector="B"/>
            </filter>
        </defs>

        <rect x="20" y="20" width="250" height="150"
            fill="orange" filter="url(#turbulenceFilter)" />
    </svg>
</body>
</html>
```

Explanation

- **<defs> and <filter>:** Similar setup as other filter examples—these elements define our reusable filter.
- **<feTurbulence>**
  - Creates the base turbulence pattern (similar to Perlin noise).
  - type="turbulence": Specifies the Perlin-like noise.
  - baseFrequency: Controls the "roughness" of the noise. Higher values mean denser detail.
  - numOctaves: Determines the layering of turbulence patterns for complexity.
  - result: Names the output of this step for later use.
- **<feDisplacementMap>**
  - Takes the turbulence ('turbulenceOutput') and uses it to displace the original graphic (SourceGraphic).
  - scale: Magnifies the displacement effect.
  - xChannelSelector, yChannelSelector: Control which color channels contribute to the displacement.
- **<rect>:**
  - The rectangle shape with filter="url(#turbulenceFilter)" applying our filter.

Key Insights

- **Abstract Effect:** Turbulence filters generate organic, distorted visuals rather than the clean-cut blur we saw previously.
- **Customization**
  - **Turbulence:** Tweak `baseFrequency` and `numOctaves` for different looks.
  - **Displacement:** Play around with the `scale` attribute.

Launch the Web page `gemini_svg_turbulence1.html` by navigating to the directory that contains this HTML Web page and then typing the following command:

```
open gemini_svg_turbulence1.html
```

After a few moments you will see an SVG rectangle rendered with an SVG turbulence filter as shown in Figure 7.11.

FIGURE 7.11. An SVG rectangle with a turbulence filter.

SVG AND CSS3 IN HTML WEB PAGES

The following prompt was supplied to Gemini in order to generate an HTML Web page with SVG-based 2D shapes and CSS3 effects.

Please generate an HTML Web page that contains SVG-based 2D shapes and CSS3 effects, along with an explanation of the code.

Gemini:
Here's a breakdown of how to combine SVG shapes with CSS3 effects to create a visually interesting composition.

Listing 7.12 displays the contents of gemini_svg_css3.html that contains Gemini-generated SVG code with CSS3 effects.

LISTING 7.12 gemini_svg_css3.html

```
<!DOCTYPE html>
<html lang="en">
<head>
    <meta charset="UTF-8">
    <meta name="viewport" content="width=device-width,
                                    initial-scale=1.0">
    <title>SVG Shapes and CSS Effects</title>
    <style>
        .shape-container {
            width: 600px;
            height: 400px;
            position: relative;
            margin: 50px auto;
        }

        .svg-shape {
            position: absolute;
        }

        #circle {
            fill: tomato;
            width: 150px;
            height: 150px;
            border-radius: 50%;
            top: 20px;
            left: 80px;
            box-shadow: 10px 15px 20px rgba(0,0,0,0.4);
        }

        #triangle {
            width: 0;
            height: 0;
            top: 120px;
            left: 350px;
            border-bottom: 120px solid lightgreen;
            border-left: 60px solid transparent;
            border-right: 60px solid transparent;
            transform: rotate(30deg);
        }

        #star {
            fill: gold;
            top: 250px;
            left: 160px;
```

```
        filter: drop-shadow(0px 5px 5px
                            rgba(0, 0, 0, 0.7));
      }
    </style>
</head>
<body>
    <div class="shape-container">
        <svg width="600" height="400">
            <circle id="circle" class="svg-shape" cx="75"
                                cy="75" r="75"  />

            <polygon id="triangle" class="svg-shape"
                     points="0,0 120,0 60,120" />

            <polygon id="star" class="svg-shape"
                points="100,10 40,198 190,78 10,78 160,198" />
        </svg>
    </div>
</body>
</html>
```

Launch the Web page gemini_svg_css3.html by navigating to the directory that contains this HTML Web page and then typing the following command:

open gemini_svg_css3.html

After a few moments you will see an SVG green circle, an SVG yellow square, and an SVG red triangle, as shown in Figure 7.12.

FIGURE 7.12. Three SVG shapes.

SVG AND JAVASCRIPT IN HTML WEB PAGES

There are several ways to render SVG in an HTML Web page, as listed in the following bullet list:

- "Pure" SVG code
- SVG and CSS3 code
- SVG and JavaScript code

You have already seen examples of the first two techniques, and the remaining code samples in this chapter show you how to use the third technique. Specifically, you will see examples of combining SVG and JavaScript to perform the following tasks:

- Render an SVG checkerboard pattern
- Render an SVG checkerboard pattern with an SVG filter
- Render a master/detail HTML Web page
- Render quadratic Bezier curves
- Render cubic Bezier curves

Recall that you have already seen SVG Filters in a previous section in this chapter.

AN SVG CHECKERBOARD PATTERN

The following prompt was supplied to Gemini in order to generate SVG-based 2D transformation effects. Please keep in mind that Gemini generated an HTML Web page that renders a 2x2 checkerboard pattern, even though the prompt explicitly asks for an 8x8 checkerboard pattern. In fact, Gemini displays the following note right after the explanation of the contents of the HTML Web page that is displayed in Listing 7.13:

```
Important Note: You'll need to add all sixty-four <rect>
elements to see the full checkerboard.  Each square has a
width/height of 60 to fit within our 480x480 viewBox.
```

```
Please generate an HTML Web page that contains an 8x8
checkerboard pattern of red and yellow rectangles whose
width is 60 and whose height is 60 that are rendered with
an SVG drop shadow, along with an explanation of the code.
```

```
Gemini:
Absolutely! Here's the HTML code to generate a checkerboard
with drop shadows using SVG, along with a breakdown of how
it works.
```

Listing 7.13 displays the contents of `gemini_svg_checkerboard1.html` that contains Gemini-generated SVG code that renders an 8x8 checkerboard pattern.

LISTING 7.13 gemini_svg_checkerboard1.html

```
<!DOCTYPE html>
<html lang="en">
<head>
    <meta charset="UTF-8">
    <meta name="viewport" content="width=device-width,
                                    initial-scale=1.0">
    <title>SVG Checkerboard</title>
    <style>
        body {
            margin: 0;
            display: flex; /* Center the SVG */
            align-items: center;
            justify-content: center;
            height: 100vh;
            background-color: #eee;
        }
        svg {
            width: 540px;
                /* Allow some space for the drop shadow */
            height: 540px;
        }
    </style>
</head>
<body>

    <svg viewBox="0 0 480 480"> <defs>
            <filter id="drop-shadow">
                <feGaussianBlur in="SourceAlpha"
                                    stdDeviation="3"/>
                <feOffset dx="4" dy="4" result="offsetblur"/>
                <feMerge>
                    <feMergeNode/>
                    <feMergeNode in="SourceGraphic"/>
                </feMerge>
            </filter>
        </defs>

        <g fill="red" filter="url(#drop-shadow)"> <rect x="0"
                        y="0" width="60" height="60" />
            <rect x="60" y="60" width="60" height="60" />
            <rect x="120" y="0" width="60" height="60" />
        </g>

        <g fill="yellow" filter="url(#drop-shadow)"> <rect
                    x="60" y="0" width="60" height="60" />
            <rect x="0" y="60" width="60" height="60" />
            <rect x="120" y="60" width="60" height="60" />
```

```
        </g>
    </svg>

</body>
</html>
```

Explanation

CSS (Centering): The CSS centers the SVG within the browser window.

SVG Structure:

viewBox: Defines the visible coordinate space (480x480 to match our checkerboard).

<defs>: Contains the filter definition for our drop shadow.

<g> Elements: We use two <g> (group) elements, one for red and one for yellow rectangles. This lets us apply the drop shadow to each color group as a whole

Drop-Shadow Filter:

<feGaussianBlur>: Creates a Gaussian blur effect.

<feOffset>: Offsets the blurred result, creating the shadow direction.

<feMerge>: Merges the shadow with the original graphic.

Rectangles in Groups:

Within each <g> we'd create the sixty-four rectangles (they were omitted for brevity).

Each <g> has the filter: url(#drop-shadow) applied.

Important Note: You'll need to add all sixty-four <rect> elements to see the full checkerboard. Each square has a width/height of 60 to fit within our 480x480 viewBox.

Launch the Web page gemini_svg_checkerboard1.html by navigating to the directory that contains this HTML Web page and then typing the following command:

```
open gemini_svg_checkerboard1.html
```

After a few moments you will see an SVG-based checkerboard pattern, as shown in Figure 7.13.

Note that Figure 7.13 displays a 2x3 checkerboard instead of an 8x8 checkerboard pattern. Let's notify Gemini and ask for updated code via the following prompt:

FIGURE 7.13. A checkerboard pattern.

The code that you generated creates a 2x3 checkerboard
pattern. Can you generate the code to render an 8x8
checkerboard pattern?

Gemini:
Absolutely, you're right! Let me provide you with the
corrected code to create a full 8x8 checkerboard. Here's
the updated HTML:

However, the new code generates a 2x8 checkerboard pattern instead of an
8x8 checkerboard pattern. This behavior (i.e., incorrect code generation) can
occur with other LLMs, perhaps due to differences in the training datasets that
are used for training different LLMs.

SUMMARY

This chapter started with a description of the strengths and weaknesses of SVG,
followed by SVG use cases, SVG accessibility, and potential security issues with
SVG. Then you saw examples of Gemini generating linear gradients, radial
gradients, and various SVG 2D shapes and gradients.

Next, you learned how to render quadratic Bezier curves and cubic Bezier
curves, as well as how to add animation effects for Bezier curves. In addition, you
saw a comparison of SVG and CSS3 as well as a comparison of SVG and PNGs.

Then you learned how to work with SVG filters, such as blur filters and
turbulence filters. You also saw code samples that combine SVG and CSS3
in an HTML Web page, as well we are combining SVG and JavaScript in an
HTML Web page.

Finally, you saw how to create other effects that involve JavaScript and
SVG, such as rendering checkerboard patterns.

INDEX

www.ingramcontent.com/pod-product-compliance
Lightning Source LLC
LaVergne TN
LVHW022118130225
803598LV00007B/98